RELIGIOUS LIFE IN AMERICA

RELIGIOUS LIFE IN AMERICA
A New Day Dawning

Seán D. Sammon, FMS

ST PAULS

Alba House

Library of Congress Cataloging-in-Publication Data

Sammon, Sean D., 1947-
    Religious life in America: a new day dawning / Sean D. Sammon.
        p. cm.
    Includes bibliographical references.
    ISBN 0-8189-0920-X (alk. paper)
    1. Monasticism and religious orders—United States. 2. Monastic and religious
life. I. Title.

BX2505 .S32 2002
255'.00973—dc21

                                                                    2002018618

Produced and designed in the United States of America by the
Fathers and Brothers of the Society of St. Paul,
2187 Victory Boulevard, Staten Island, New York 10314-6603,
as part of their communications apostolate.

ISBN: 0-8189-0920-X

Printing Information:

Current Printing - first digit   2   3   4   5   6   7   8   9   10

Year of Current Printing - first year shown

                2004   2005   2006   2007   2008   2009   2010

Dedication

With thanks to my Marist brothers.

TABLE
OF
CONTENTS

INTRODUCTION

Another book about apostolic religious life in the United States! Over the past four decades, haven't we had more than our fill of them? Some were hopeful and encouraging, others pessimistic and disheartening. All were trying to make sense of a way of life whose future appears increasingly uncertain.

In this book, I invite you to join me in taking another look at consecrated life in the U.S. Despite the diminishments of the last 40 years, I forecast a hopeful future for it and for a number of congregations in the States. With what justification? Actually, there are two. The first is Jesus, who will always be worthy of the total gift of self that is at the heart of religious life.

The second is my belief that the hard work involved in revitalizing our way of life is just now moving into a new phase in the U.S. Yes, though darkness and uncertainty have plagued us on our almost 40-year-long pilgrimage of renewal, this conviction is growing among many of us: a new day is dawning once again for consecrated life in this country.

A ray of light: the growing number of men and women religious interested in laying the groundwork for a renewed form of consecrated life aimed at transforming our world.[1] Eager to engage that world so as to evangelize it, we are keen to commit ourselves to an explicit life of prayer, the proclamation of God's Word, and communities that witness to reconciliation and peace.[2]

Make no mistake about it: we have little interest in a nostalgic restoration of a pre-conciliar style of our way of life. For us, however, religious life is God's work and not a human project.[3]

Sunrise and sunset are essential parts of each day. Both are also integral to the history of consecrated life. No surprise, then, that during the past four decades our once familiar and predictable way of life fell apart. Sociologist Patricia Wittberg, SC, observes that declines in membership and in the viability of religious orders have occurred regularly over the centuries.[4] In the wake of the French Revolution, for example, the membership of congregations fell dramatically. In 1789, there were approximately 2,000 Benedictine establishments in Europe. By 1815, a mere 26 years later, only 20 were still functioning.[5] Similarly, prior to that same Revolution the number of men religious in Europe totaled 300,000; by 1830 that figure had fallen to 70,000, a decline of more than 75 percent in just over 40 years.[6]

And yet, another day dawned and an amazing revival of consecrated life followed. Over the next 150 years more new congregations were founded than during any comparable period in the history of our Church.[7] About 600 alone came into existence during the 19th century.[8] Some older orders also grew again in membership and vitality.[9] The Jesuits, for example, suppressed from 1773 until 1814, flourished as never before.[10]

In suggesting that "a new day is dawning in America" for religious life, I cannot deny this fact: we will create our future from a position of poverty rather than abundance. Our groups are, after all, smaller and older, and lack the clear sense of identity they possessed in the past. What, then, is the primary challenge that we face today? To decide whether we have the faith, the hope, and the passion to bring to life the future that God has in mind for our way of life.

In this book, I identify and describe some of the difficult decisions that we will have to make if our way of life and its mission are to remain vital in the U.S. as a new century gets underway. My purpose, however, is not to ensure the survival of consecrated life as we know it. If history repeats itself, we can reasonably expect that some congregations will die out in the not too distant future. This outcome has been a part of every major transition in the history of religious life: in patristic times, in the Middle Ages, in the period of the Reformation, and, as mentioned earlier, in the aftermath of the French Revolution.[11]

Other congregations will enter into a long period of low-level or minimal survival.[12] In the past, some larger groups shrank in size and remained small until their fundamental spirit and our Church's spirituality once again became congruent.[13] Trappist monasteries, for example, largely overlooked for years by the great majority of U.S. Catholics, have in recent times been redis-covered due to renewed interest in the contemplative dimension of Christian life.

Still other congregations will experience a transforming re-birth during the years just ahead. The members of these groups are occupied presently with profound and troubling questions about religious life and its meaning. These efforts will lead them to answers radical enough to bring about the revitalization for which we all long.[14]

But the rebirth of our congregations will call for more than our personal conversion. Together, we must also interact with our Church and the wider world. And, since religious life's pre-dominant image is itself shifting today, congregations founded for service in the 19th century must reinterpret their ministries in light of our Church's current needs and an accurate reading of the signs of our times.[15]

In addition to an *Introduction,* this book has eight chapters and an *Epilogue.* In the first chapter, *Getting from There to Here,* you are invited to relive the history of U.S. religious life from the early 1950's until the present, and examine briefly its current situation. These two points are emphasized throughout Chapter I: one, religious life lost its identity at Vatican II; and, two, it was not provided with a satisfactory new one. Thus, though not the intention of those who participated in that historic meeting, some of their decisions helped contribute to almost four decades of unraveling among sisters, religious priests, and brothers in this country.[16]

The second chapter, *Revitalization: Reading the Tea Leaves,* centers on this question: Do you and I believe that a revitalization of U.S. religious life is possible today? After all, isn't that the crux of the matter? We will examine past periods of upheaval in consecrated life, assuming that earlier alternating patterns of decline and revitalization may very well repeat themselves today.

In the third chapter, *A Fork in the Road,* we take a look at the identity of religious life in the States today. Let's start by asking this question: What makes our life different from other equally valid ways of living out the Gospel? In recent years, many believers have been hard pressed to identify anything much that differentiates women and men religious from everyone else. However, if consecrated life is not somehow distinct, unique, and challenging, why would a person embrace it? Hasn't the time come for us to agree upon a fresh and compelling identity for our way of life?

Chapter IV, *Persona and Purpose,* and the two chapters that follow it, offer some suggestions about how to describe religious life in a post-conciliar U.S. Church. Throughout these chapters, two points are stressed. In the first place, no matter its past or future form, apostolic religious life will always be marked by three distinct characteristics: ministry, community, and spirituality. Secondly, consecrated life, in any form whatsoever, must be worth the gift of one's life.

Mission and Ministry, so central to the identity of each of our congregations, are addressed in Chapter IV. When we come right down to it, isn't evangelization our only mission? Our life's work is to love God and to make God known and loved. Whether our ministry is health care, carpentry, education, social work, cooking, or any of a thousand and one other possible labors, the mission of each of us is to be *Good News* in word and deed.

In Chapter V, *Re-Imagining Community Life*, we examine another necessary element for a U.S. religious life that is vital and viable for the 21st century: community. The often mechanical and almost solely work-driven communities of the past no longer appeal to most of us who are midlife and senior religious. Not surprisingly, they have little attraction for the young. Neither does life alone in an apartment. In Chapter V, I ask and answer two questions: Can we create religious communities in which members flourish, rather than just survive? And, if so, what might they look like?

Chapter VI, *Spirituality: Turn on Your Heart Lights*, focuses on the person who must be at the center of contemporary consecrated life: Jesus Christ. The real crises today among those of us who are men and women religious are not related to vocations. They concern spirituality and meaning. Without Jesus as its center and regular personal and communal prayer as part of its pattern, our way of life will very quickly make little sense to us, or to anyone else.

Early in the sixth chapter, I make two points: one, the spirituality and ways of prayer among those of us in apostolic congregations must reflect the heritage of our groups; and, two, they must also have their roots in the marketplace. Simply put, our spirituality and practice of prayer must be part of all the activities of our life. Over the last four decades, in our attempts to stretch and deepen our understanding and experience of both, however, we have often failed to move away from a spirituality and style of praying more appropriate to the daily rhythm of the monastery. Isn't it about time for a change?

The seventh chapter, *Fresh Faces at the Breakfast Table,* and the eighth, *Last Call for Religious Life,* introduce the topic of vocations to our way of life among young people in the U.S. today. If we are to welcome a new morning for religious life in the States, then we will need some fresh faces at the breakfast table. These chapters offer strategies for improving the ways in which we promote vocations.

We begin by taking a look at a group of Americans known as Generation X. The discussion explores these questions: Who are the members of this group? What is their relationship to our Church? Is their image of religious life positive or not?

Unfortunately, many of those who have written about Xers to date have focused primarily on upwardly mobile young men and women who enjoy a certain economic advantage. Their working class brothers and sisters among all races and ethnic groups, and including young people new to this country, are notable in the discussion by their absence. Vocations to religious life in the U.S. have, in the past, come primarily from the families of the working class. The hopes, dreams, fears, concerns, and beliefs of young Catholic working class women and men, therefore, are touched upon in Chapter VII.

We will also take a look at a younger and currently emerging group, known popularly as Generation Y or the Millennial Generation. Born between 1982 and the early years of the 21st century, many of these young people may, in fact, have greater interest in joining religious life than the men and women who make up the group that has gone just ahead of them. The members of the Millennial Generation have benefited from stronger and more effective programs of religious education and young adult ministry developed in recent years. They have also profited from greater emphasis being placed on children, a slowing in the rise of the divorce rate, and a renewed interest in religious issues.[17]

An *Epilogue,* integrating several ideas discussed in the book and examining the challenges faced by leaders in religious congregations in the United States, completes the text.

We have on hand today an abundance of articles and books about consecrated life. Many do a fine job of analyzing our current situation and identifying the challenges that we face in the task of renewing and adapting our way of life. What we also need at the moment, however, are manuals that will help us apply concretely all that we have learned over the past 40 years about re-imagining consecrated life for the 21st century. Our challenge? To reclaim the values that lie at the heart of our way of living the Gospel and to express them in new form.

This book, while hardly a manual, is practical in nature: it offers specific recommendations about what might be done to further the renewal of religious congregations in the U.S. Neither agreement nor consensus is the expected outcome here. Rather, I put forward these recommendations to foster further discussion and, hopefully, action that will advance the process of renewal. The reflection questions that appear at the end of each chapter are one means for achieving that goal. I encourage you to share your responses with members of your community as well as with a wider circle of people with an interest in consecrated life and its future in this country.

Contemporary religious life is just now emerging from a period that has been both blessed and burdensome. Those of us who are its members continue to face some formidable and complex challenges. The work that lies ahead will require of us open minds, a willingness to surrender divisive ideological points of view, and a great deal of sacrifice.

In *The Heretical Imperative,*[18] sociologist Peter Berger explores an important task confronting all Christians today: to discern and decide what to select from our inheritance of the past and our experiences in the present. To help us avoid pitfalls in carrying out this responsibility, Berger identifies two false responses: a rigid attempt to recapture and restore the past, and total capitulation to the present.

As men and women religious, we face the same challenge today: bringing out of our store the new *and* the old, in the spirit of *both/and* rather than *either/or*. As we address this task, we must rely both on the God of our experience and the God of our memory, on the One who is and the One who has brought us to where we are today. We must also rely on the God who is to come, the God of hope, since our concern is about the future of consecrated life in the U.S. May that God — the God who was, who is, and who is to come — surprise us all with what is in store for religious life now that it has entered a new century.[19]

My fondest hope is that this book will serve as an incentive for continuing the conversation about U.S. religious life and its need for transformation. That discussion got underway well before Pope John XXIII convened a remarkable Council called Vatican II and set a new direction for our Church. May his vision and boldness be an inspiration to us all as we work together to renew consecrated life for this time in history.

No book comes to life without the work of many hands. This one is no exception to that rule. I am grateful to my Marist Brothers Patrick Bignell, Gerard Brereton, Aidan Bridge, Robert Clark, Dennis Cooper, Jeff Crowe, Fernand Dostie, Richard Dunleavy, Mark Field, Michael Flanigan, José Angel Henríquez, Ken Hogan, James Jolley, John J. Malich, John McDonnell, Joseph McKee, Roy Mooney, Brendan O'Shea, Dominic O'Sullivan, Jude Pieterse, Hank Sammon, Leo Shea, Anthony Shears, Allen Sherry, Brian Sweeney, and Leonard Voegtle, as well as Sister Cathy Bertrand, SSND, Rev. Frederick Bliss, SM, Brother Paul Hennessy, CFC, John E. Kerrigan, Jr., Sister Rea McDonnell, SSND, John and Margaret Perring-Mulligan, Ronald Pasquariello, and Mary Sammon who read drafts of the manuscript, and made many helpful suggestions for change. If the book is clear in its message and helpful to the reader, they deserve the credit. The author is, of course, responsible for any misconceptions or errors that exist in the text.

Several other people helped the author see this book through to completion. A word of thanks to Brother Benito Arbués, FMS, Superior General. During the past seven years that we have shared ministry and life together, he has so often encouraged me to write. I am particularly grateful for his support as this book came to life.

Editors are special people. A word of gratitude to Sister Marie Kraus, SNDdeN, and Ronald Pasquariello. The care with which they applied their editorial red pens to this text, coupled with their skill at dusting clutter from sentence and paragraph alike, clarified many points in the book and rendered it more comprehensible.

Thanks, too, to Rev. Edmund Lane, SSP, my editor at Alba House, whose interest in this project motivated me to get on with the task of writing. I am grateful to him for shepherding this book through all the stages of its development.

Special thanks to Brother Fernand Dostie, FMS, my colleague, fellow Marist Brother, and friend. Throughout the writing of this book, he has been enthusiastic in his support. He will, I know, celebrate its completion. Thanks, Dostie, for being there with your wit and wisdom when mine were on the wane!

Some parts of the text first appeared, in somewhat different form, in *Human Development* magazine. I am grateful to Rev. James Gill, SJ and Linda Amadeo at *HD* for their permission to reproduce that material here.

This book is dedicated to my almost 5,000 Marist Brothers worldwide. I have been privileged to be part of this religious community of men for thirty-five years now. While I have had my share of questions and doubts along the way, I really cannot imagine spending my life in any other way.

The fidelity of my brothers to the vision of our recently canonized founder, Marcellin Champagnat, and their love and support of young people, particularly the poor among them, as well as the love and support they have given me so freely, have inspired and encouraged me for more than three decades now. I am very grateful. Believing, as I do, that a new day is dawning for religious life in the U.S. today, I look forward to working together with them as we strive to re-imagine and bring to birth Marist life for the 21st century.

> Seán D. Sammon, FMS
> Rome, Italy
> 6 June 2001
> Feast of Saint Marcellin Champagnat

Notes

[1] Paul Philibert, OP, "Toward a Transformative Model of Religious Life," *Origins* 29:1 (May 20, 1999), 9-14.

[2] Carolyn Osiek, "A woman stands at Mount Nebo," *National Catholic Reporter* 36:16 (February 18, 2000), 22-23.

[3] Albert Dilanni, "Vocations: New Signs of the Times," *Forum Novum* 5:1 (May 2000), 5-10.

[4] Patricia Wittberg, *The Rise and Fall of Catholic Religious Orders: A Social Movement Perspective* (New York: The State University of New York Press, 1994), 40.

[5] John Padberg, "The Contexts of Comings and Goings," in Laurie Felknor, ed., *The Crisis in Religious Vocations* (Mahwah, NJ: Paulist Press, 1989), 22.

[6] Albert Dilanni, "Religious Life: Directions for a Future," *Review for Religious* 55:4 (July/August 1996), 342-364.

[7] Padberg, "The Contexts of Comings and Goings," 22.

[8] Lawrence Cada and Raymond Fitz, Gertrude Foley, Thomas Giardino, and Carol Lichtenberg, *Shaping the Coming Age of Religious Life* (Whitinsville, MA: Affirmation Books, 1985), 39.

[9] Ibid., 40.

[10] Dilanni, "Religious Life: Directions for a Future," 344.

[11] John Manuel Lozano, "Religious Life: the Continuing Journey—Vision and Hope," in Cassian J. Yuhaus, CP, ed., *Religious Life: the Challenge for Tomorrow* (Mahwah, NJ: Paulist Press, 1994), 143-161.

Introduction

12 Cada, et. al., *Shaping the Coming Age of Religious Life,* 59.

13 Lozano, "Religious Life: the Continuing Journey—Vision and Hope," 159-160.

14 Cada, et. al., *Shaping the Coming Age of Religious Life,* 88.

15 Lozano, "Religious Life: the Continuing Journey—Vision and Hope," 159-160.

16 David L. Fleming, "Understanding a Theology of Religious Life," in Gerald A. Arbuckle and David L. Fleming, eds., *Religious Life: Rebirth through Conversion* (Staten Island, NY: Alba House, 1990), 32-49; See also Paul Molinari and Peter Gumpel, *Chapter VI of the Dogmatic Constitution "Lumen Gentium" on Religious Life* (Rome: Università Gregoriana, 1987).

17 NCCB Committee on Vocations, *Summary of Vocations Research,* http://www.nccbuscc.org/voctions/resrch/summary 1.

18 Peter Berger, *The Heretical Imperative* (New York: Anchor Press/Doubleday, 1979).

19 Gerald O'Collins, *Experiencing Jesus* (London: Society for Promoting Christian Knowledge, 1994), 1-9.

Chapter 1

GETTING FROM THERE TO HERE

What does it take to be a religious—sister, brother, or priest—in the United States today? Tremendous faith and a willingness to take action! Many U.S. Catholics, including a number of men and women religious, are troubled about the state of contemporary consecrated life and its future. How could we not be: the total number of sisters and brothers in the States has dropped more than 50 percent over the past 35 years.[1]

The figures on those joining our ranks are hardly reassuring. In the 1960's, for example, approximately 7,000 candidates per year entered religious orders of women in this country, accounting for 17 percent of their annual membership. By 1981, however, less than four percent of all sisters each year were new recruits; by 1990, they constituted less than one percent.[2]

The ever-decreasing number of young women religious in the U.S. suggests that the long-standing and steady falling off in the number of entrants to most religious congregations continues unabated.[3] This pattern of decline comes at a time when people expected the young adults of the baby boom generation to provide a larger than normal pool of applicants for our way of life in the United States.

We have experienced the graying of religious life. As 1997 came to a close, for example, less than three percent of women religious were below age 40, while more than 70 percent were 60 years old or more.[4] But, in 1999, there were as many sisters over age 70 as under.[5] Current statistics on men religious, while not so alarming, are hardly encouraging: approximately 43 percent are below age 60.[6]

What is happening in other parts of our world? In some countries, the overall picture mirrors that of the States. Candidates entering the major German seminaries decreased from 744 in 1979 to 279 in 1995.[7] The number of postulants joining congregations of women religious in Great Britain also fell steadily from the decade's high of 62 in 1990 to 27 in 1997. In 1990, 95 men began the process of formation for the brotherhood in Britain; seven years later the number of new candidates entering annually fell by a third.[8] Similar trends have been reported for Italy, France, the Netherlands, and other nations of Western Europe.

Many religious are consoled by their congregation's growth in sub-Saharan Africa and parts of Asia, especially India and Indonesia.[9] In 1999, for example, U.S. Jesuits reported a total of 96 first and second year novices. Among Indian Jesuits, however, there were more than three times those numbers of novices for the same year.[10]

There are other troubling signs of decline in consecrated life in the United States. A number of congregational leaders report that a significant proportion of their time is taken up with matters of diminution: aging membership, retirement issues, nursing care, the closing of long-standing institutions.

All these developments have helped foster an attitude of resignation among some U.S. Catholics, including a number of men and women religious. They have come to believe that, while consecrated life may be flourishing in other parts of our world, it is undoubtedly dying in the United States. Hasn't the time come, they ask, to settle the poor soul's debts, distribute its remaining assets, insure the care of its aged members, and let this way of life die with dignity? We can console ourselves in our loss, they tell us, with the hope that someday in the future, religious life will emerge and thrive once again.

With all that said, however, we must also acknowledge that some congregations in the U.S. are attracting vocations, and in numbers significant enough to be noticed. Writing as early as 1993, Albert DiIanni, SM, then Vicar General for the Marist Fathers, confessed to being perplexed by the following situation: as members of a number of long-standing apostolic congregations bemoaned their lack of candidates, one Roman seminary of the Legionaries of Christ housed 290 young men, eager to work in any part of the world to which obedience might send them.[11]

While numbers are not the be-all and end-all measure of a religious congregation's state of health, we cannot ignore the fact that hundreds of other young people also are entering congregations such as Mother Teresa's missioners, the Daughters of Saint Paul, the Oblates of the Blessed Virgin Mary, and the Brothers of Saint John. Still others are joining one or another of the many new lay movements in Europe: Rome's Community of San Egidio, the Focolari, the Neocatechumenate, the Opus Dei, and so forth.

In seeking some explanation for these developments, DiIanni asks two questions: Is this situation an anomaly? Can the vocational decisions of all these young people be dismissed simply as the end result of a search for security?[12]

DiIanni makes two other points clear: he is not advocating that other religious congregations imitate these prospering groups, nor is he urging them to seek vocations from these new lay movements, varied as they are. What we need to do is find out why young people in our highly secularized society are attracted in such numbers to these groups.[13]

Inevitable outcomes

The belief that religious life is on life support has serious consequences. Judging these to be its last days, for example, many Catholics hesitate to invite young women and men to consider religious life as a vocation. Others ask, "Why join a religious congregation during the 'age of the laity'?" One need not be a sister, religious priest, or brother, they point out, to take up a ministry in the Church today.

Three tasks are necessary to ensure that our way of living the Gospel remains vital in the U.S. Church. They are clarifying its identity, boldly implementing its adaptation and renewal, and promoting vocations.

Suppose that this observation—that U.S. consecrated life is dying—is merely a misperception? More to the point, what would happen to our ways of thinking and behaving if we were to accept as valid the premise that religious life in this country is on the brink of rebirth? How would we feel and act? What message would we give to young people?

In the beginning

The seismic changes that have shaken religious life in the U.S. since Vatican II got underway well in advance of the first session of that landmark Council. In late 1950, for example, the then-existing Sacred Congregation for Religious convened in Rome its first General Assembly of religious. About 4,000 superiors and other congregational representatives heard Pius XII encourage them to modify dated and nonessential customs and to adapt their excessively strict cloister restrictions. The group eventually reached agreement on three fundamental criteria for renewal: "great fidelity to the Founder [or Foundress], to venerable traditions, and to preserving the particular spirit of each Institute."[14]

A year later the Pope repeated the same message at a gathering of teaching sisters, and urged those present to provide their members with professional training equal to that of their lay counterparts. U.S. sisters as a group responded quickly to these challenges. During a national congress held in 1952 at the University of Notre Dame, they focused their attention on the professional and spiritual education of the young women entering their congregations. Up until that time, a significant number of religious sisters and brothers were assigned teaching responsibilities prior to completing the requirements for their bachelor's degree. This policy caused some U.S. citizens to criticize Catholic schools as educationally inferior institutions staffed by inadequately prepared teachers.

In the same year, a panel discussion at the annual meeting of the National Catholic Educational Association also addressed the Pope's remarks to teaching sisters. As a result of this exchange, the leadership of women's congregations in the United States made a decision to survey their membership so as to identify obstacles to providing the type of education for which the Pope was calling.

The survey's findings brought to light three concerns. First of all, the time required to complete an undergraduate degree appeared prohibitive when measured against the ever-increasing demand, on the part of pastors and bishops, for sisters to teach in a steadily expanding Catholic school system. Next, the cost of education far outstripped what the meager stipends provided to women religious at the time could support. Finally, the study's results found a lack of understanding among the clergy and a number of sisters as to the necessity of a more protracted period of study.[15]

Quickly responding to the investigation's findings, U.S. women religious established, in 1954, the Sisters Formation Conference. Thanks to this organization, American sisters became the most highly educated group of women religious in the Catholic Church, and among the most highly educated groups of women in the United States.[16] The Sisters Formation Conference would also later be described (by Lora Ann Quinonez, CDP, at one time Executive Director of the Leadership Conference of Women Religious, and Mary Daniel Turner, SNDdeN, a past-President of the same organization) as "the single most critical ground for the radical transformative process" in religious life that took place after Vatican II.[17]

Another landmark year was 1956. Prodded by Vatican authorities, the superiors of U.S. men and women's religious congregations established two national associations: the Conference of Major Superiors of Men (CMSM) and the Conference of Major Superiors of Women (CMSW). Though evidence exists that one national conference was thought of originally, women religious, pointing to the concentration of their membership in one apostolate, education, and wary lest control of a single national body end up disproportionately in the hands of its male members, pressed for two organizations.[18]

By the end of the 1950's, then, a broad-based organizational structure was in place to help religious congregations in the U.S. address the educational and spiritual reforms suggested ten years earlier by Pius XII. However, while the Pope had called for significant changes in religious life's day-to-day expression, at no time did he question the underlying ideological framework on which it was based. In his 1954 encyclical *Sacra Virginitas*, for example, Pius XII continued to describe virginity and consecrated life as superior to marriage for achieving holiness. The Catholic Church had held this position since the time of Origen in the third century.

Looking ahead to a new decade, we religious had a sense of well-being. The identity of our way of life was clear. The quality of religious formation programs was steadily improving, and closer ties had been established among our congregational leaders. Catholic schools and hospitals were expanding in number and range of services, and many young men and women were entering our novitiates. The future of U.S. religious life, measured by the standards of the day,[19] looked very bright indeed.

However, this situation was soon to change. Unaware of the long-term impact of their vote, the bishops who gathered for Vatican II would, within a short while, approve documents that questioned the ideological foundation on which eighteen centuries of Roman Catholic consecrated life had been built.[20] By their decisions, they would also unknowingly help set into motion almost four decades of upheaval among the members of congregations in the United States.

Vatican II's impact

As a result of decisions made at Vatican II, women and men religious lost not only their familiar identity, but also consequently, a strong sense of who they were or where they were going.[21] Unfortunately, many of the Council participants, as well as the vast majority of us, failed at the time to realize that fact.

While the loss of consecrated life's pre-conciliar identity was, in the judgment of many, a positive development, the failure of Council participants to lay a foundation on which to build a new identity for our way of life was regrettable. This omission contributed, in part, to a now well-known outcome: years of conflict and confusion about the place and purpose of religious life in today's Church. To understand more fully the state of contemporary U.S. religious life and the challenges it faces, then, we need first to answer this question: *Just how did consecrated life in the States get to where it is today?*

John XXIII, calling on Catholics to let some fresh air into the Church, officially opened the Second Vatican Council on October 11, 1962. It was the first ecumenical council held in almost 100 years, and the majority of those participating were determined to move the Church beyond the neo-scholastic world in which it found itself.

When it came to deciding how best to accomplish this task, however, the Council's participants followed generally two streams of thought. One group adopted a *back to basics* or *reformist*[22] point of view. Suspicious of modernity and cautious about new theological currents, it restrictively grounded change in the earlier stages of Church tradition. This group wanted to rediscover tradition and live it anew.[23]

But a second group of participants was *pro-change.* They advocated a new kind of Church: one that would integrate into itself the modern world's best insights. Their approach to change was *revolutionary.* Broadly speaking, while the members of the first group looked more to *Lumen Gentium,* the Council's Dogmatic Constitution on the Church, for direction, those in the second identified closely with the spirit of *Gaudium et Spes,* Vatican II's Pastoral Constitution on the Church in the Modern World. They were determined to integrate the joys and hopes, and the grief and anguish of humanity into the life of each Christian.

Unfortunately, the back to basics and pro-change points-of-view were never fully integrated at Vatican II, but remained juxtaposed. With what result? The Council Fathers failed, in general, to arrive at an overall unified teaching, one that they could call their own.[24] The document they produced on the adaptation and renewal of religious life, *Perfectae Caritatis,* is a case in point. It reflected both the *back to basics* and the *pro-change* points of view. Men and women religious were encouraged to return to such foundational elements as their congregation's charism and the original vision of their founder or foundress. At the same time, they were instructed to read the signs of the times and to act accordingly. These two fundamentally different approaches to renewal, in time, gave rise to confusion and conflict among us religious, and between us and a number of diocesan priests, members of the hierarchy, and lay men and women.

    Lumen Gentium, rather than *Perfectae Caritatis,* eventually was to have more importance for our way of life. From the early Middle Ages until Vatican II, most Catholics accepted unchallenged a three-tiered hierarchical ranking of the clerical, religious, and lay states within the Church. While appropriately characterized as "popular theology," this model led the majority of Catholics to understand that priesthood was the "highest calling" in terms of a vocation. The religious life came second. Catholics were taught that only vowed members of religious orders could achieve spiritual perfection. The lay state, unfortunately, ranked a distant third. Many lay men and women, not called to priesthood or religious life, felt like second-class citizens in their own Church.

    The fifth chapter of *Lumen Gentium* turned the three-tiered hierarchical model on its head. It declared that all Church members, *by virtue of their baptism,* receive an equal call "to the fullness of the Christian life and the perfection of charity."[25] With this simple sentence, the Council Fathers put aside the ideology upon which religious life had been based for centuries. Consecrated life, they declared, "from the point of view of the divine and hierarchical nature of the Church, [was no longer] to be seen as a middle way between clerical and lay states of life. Rather it should be seen as a way of life to which some Christians are called by God, both from the clergy and the laity."[26]

Identity crisis for religious life

In retrospect, we realize that Vatican II faced forthrightly the necessary and urgent challenge of defining the rightful place of lay men and women within the Church community. It was, however, less successful in its attempt to redefine clearly the nature and purpose of consecrated life. *Perfectae Caritatis* fell far short of advancing for religious the type of groundbreaking theology that *Lumen Gentium* had done for the laity. Coming to life in a difficult and complex way, the Council's document on the adaptation and renewal of religious life was assured promulgation only after personal intervention by Paul VI.[27]

The Pope's input took the form of a May 1964 address, entitled *Magno gaudio,* in which he set about to clarify the identity of religious life. He touched on several topics: the primacy of the spiritual life, fidelity to the original traditions of each congregation, the place and role of religious in the Church, a conciliar understanding of the evangelical counsels, the apostolate and relations with the hierarchy. Of special significance for any future efforts to clarify religious life's identity was Paul VI's insistence that the universal call to holiness was not to be seen as prejudicial to the religious state.[28]

Despite this initiative and others, in the minds of many people, our way of life emerged from the Council weakened. Without its prior and long-standing identity, it seemed no longer to have a clear place within the Church community. Consequently, religious life found itself facing some uncertain and difficult dilemmas. *Gaudium et Spes,* for example, proclaimed the Church to be in solidarity with the world. As religious, many of us were now confronted with the challenge of making peace with the very world that for centuries we had been taught to shun.

The role of religious priests was also unclear. Was priesthood their primary identity, or was it religious life? The Council document on religious life lacked any theology of religious priesthood that clearly distinguished its members from their diocesan counterparts.[29]

Perfectae Caritatis sent out other confusing signals. Consider what it had to say about the vow of obedience. On the one hand, the dignity of the person was to be respected; on the other, "the superior's authority to decide on what must be done and to require the doing of it"[30] was not to be weakened. Wittberg suggests that these two different points of view led, in later years, to a number of predictable conflicts.[31]

The second paragraph of article 10 of *Perfectae Caritatis* was also a source of confusion for many religious brothers from lay congregations. It stated, in part, that there was "nothing to prevent some members of institutes of brothers being admitted to holy orders—the lay character of their institutes remaining intact—by provision of their general chapter and in order to meet the need for priestly ministration in their houses."[32]

The text appears neither to encourage nor discourage the introduction of the priesthood into brothers' congregations. Cardinal Antoniutti, the Prefect of the Sacred Congregation for Religious, had a firm opinion. When addressing General Chapters of brothers' congregations shortly after the Council's final session, he strayed from his prepared text on more than one occasion and insisted that it was the will of the Holy Father that the priesthood be introduced.[33] Only a few congregations of brothers took his recommendation to heart. Among those that did, some eventually regretted doing so.

The Conciliar document on the adaptation and renewal of religious life, *Perfectae Caritatis,* failed to provide it with a clear and unambiguous identity. Even the document's title gave a mixed message, seeming to suggest, once again, that our way of life was more perfect than that of a lay man or woman. The fact that *Lumen Gentium* had only recently defined brothers and sisters as members of the laity added to the confusion.

As we embarked upon the process of renewing religious life and adapting it to the modern age, we had little in the way of specific directions to guide us. Vatican II had suppressed the conventional ideological foundation for our way of life, and had failed to provide us with a new one. Unfortunately, during the years ahead, these limitations were to be the source of many painful misunderstandings, confrontations, and conflicts among the members of individual religious communities, and between a number of us and some lay Catholics, diocesan priests, segments of the hierarchy, and Vatican authorities. Strife appeared to have quickly become part of Vatican II's legacy.

The seeds of future problems

The seeds of other problems were also unintentionally sown about this time. The Council participants recommended a renewal process that had the Gospel at its heart and was based on the charism and spirit of each congregation's founder or foundress. This approach served to encourage a measure of independence among us in undertaking renewal and, at least in word, did not appear averse to our taking a variety of approaches to this task. Implementing this directive, however, led—in keeping with aspects of the culture—to pluralism and unconstrained initiatives on the part of some religious congregations. These characteristics were not what bishops and others in Church leadership had come to expect from sisters, religious priests, and brothers in the United States.

Paul VI, in *Ecclesiae Sanctae II,* did lay down some general guidelines for adapting and renewing religious life subsequent to the Council. He pointed out, for example, that "it [was] the institutes themselves that [had] the main responsibility for renewal and adaptation,"[34] and went on to say "that they shall accomplish this especially by means of general chapters."[35] These chapters were given the right to "alter, temporarily, certain prescriptions of the constitutions… by way of experiment, provided that the purpose, nature and character of the institute [was] safeguarded."[36] In keeping with the mind of Paul VI, the Vatican Congregation for Religious and Secular Institutes, during the years just after the Council, maintained a policy of discreet non-directive involvement when it came to the implementation of renewal.[37]

The Pope continued to write and speak about religious life, and left an outstanding body of teachings on the subject. *Evangelica Testificatio* proved to be his *Magna Carta* for the renewal of consecrated life according to the mind of Vatican II. He once described it as among the most important documents of his pontificate. During his remaining years as Pope, Paul VI continually returned to these themes when he addressed women and men religious: the primacy of the spiritual life, the appropriate renewal of constitutions with total and generous fidelity to the mind of the Church, the preservation of wholesome traditions, faithfulness to the spirit of the foundress or founder, fidelity to the charism of the Institute, the following of Christ in a state consecrated to God, an apostolate proper to the Institute, and the scope and function of the General Chapter in achieving these aims.

But the Pope was not naïve; he was well aware of the difficulties involved in adapting and renewing religious life. In *Evangelica Testificatio,* he wrote, "Religious life, if it is to be renewed, must adapt its accidental forms… not by abandoning its true identity, but in asserting itself in the vitality that is its own. It is a sublime task in the measure that it is a difficult one."[38] Men and women religious, working to renew their congregations, could only agree. In theory, the directives included in *Perfectae Caritatis* and *Ecclesiae Sanctae II* appeared to be simple and straightforward. But in practice, the obligations that these documents placed on all institutes, their General Chapters, and superiors were quite complex.

The Sisters' Survey

The Conference of Major Superiors of Women (CMSW) acted quickly to get the process of adaptation and renewal underway. Their President at the time, Mary Luke Tobin, SL, had been the sole U.S. woman religious to serve as an auditor at the Council during its 1964 and 1965 sessions. To help them in their work, the Conference leadership engaged the services of Marie Augusta Neal, SNDdeN, a sociologist on the faculty of Boston's Emmanuel College. The task before her was clear-cut but challenging: design and administer a survey of the entire membership of all congregations with representation in CMSW.

A 23-page, 649-question survey was sent out to 157,000 professed sisters in the United States. Despite its length, 88 percent of those who received this mailing responded. Obviously, this instrument gathered a significant amount of valuable data about U.S. women religious and their thinking. What was unexpected, however, was the way in which the survey itself raised the consciousness of some who completed it. For example, asking a sister if she had read the works of a particular modern theologian also suggested to her that this task was a legitimate undertaking. A number of respondents began to embark on activities that they might otherwise not have thought about doing on their own.[39]

While the survey's results were being collected and analyzed, some congregations held the extraordinary General Chapters that the Vatican decree had called for so as to move renewal along. In one far-reaching example, on October 16, 1967, the Immaculate Heart Sisters of Los Angeles announced that they would gradually introduce a wide-ranging set of changes in their rule and way of life.[40] Sisters were to have a greater number of options from which to choose the clothes they wore, and the members of each convent would henceforth be free to determine the kind of local government they wanted. Cardinal James McIntyre, the local Archbishop, reacted immediately. He demanded that the sisters reverse their Chapter decisions or else withdraw from the 31 Archdiocesan schools that they staffed.

The sisters' refusal to follow the Archbishop's orders precipitated a papal investigation in 1968. As a result of that procedure, Cardinal Antoniutti, the Prefect of the Sacred Congregation for Religious, wrote to the leaders of all U.S. congregations and dismissed the changes initiated by the sisters in California as contrary to religious life. The IHM community was ordered to retain a uniform dress or religious habit, continue in their traditional apostolate of teaching, and obey the bishop.

Reacting to the standoff between Cardinal McIntyre and the Immaculate Heart Sisters, some communities of U.S. religious issued public statements in support of the sisters. By March 1968, at least 3,000 women religious had signed a public petition supporting the IHMs in their "battle" against the Cardinal. Shortly thereafter, 194 prominent educators, artists, writers, and members of the clergy forwarded a letter to Pope Paul VI urging freedom for the sisters to "experiment." Numbered among the signers were such notables of the period as theologians Harvey Cox, Rosemary Ruether, and Reinhold Niebuhr, as well as Arthur

15

Lichtenberger, the retired presiding bishop of the Episcopal Church.[41]

Meeting in National Assembly in 1969, the membership of the Conference of Major Superiors of Women (CMSW) also passed a resolution of support. Father Edward Heston attended the gathering as the representative of the Sacred Congregation for Religious. He insisted that the needs of a religious community must take second place to the local bishop's directives, and that the guidance of the hierarchy in the process of renewal must be accepted. He was generally ignored.

A small group participating in the Assembly was upset by this reaction on the part of the larger body. They judged it to be disrespectful and a direct affront to the Church's legitimate authority over religious life. These sisters shortly thereafter withdrew from CMSW and formed the nucleus of an organization of U.S. women religious called "Consortium Perfectae Caritatis."

And what happened to the Immaculate Heart congregation in Los Angeles? It eventually divided into two groups: one made up of 455 of its mainly younger members, and another composed of about 50 of its older sisters. Those in the first group, led by Anita Caspary, were committed to continue experimenting with renewal; members of the second group preferred to follow the directives of the Archbishop. The first group was forced by the Vatican to dissolve as a recognized religious congregation. The letter instructing them to do so was described by one observer as legal and frigid, and completely devoid of any words of appreciation for the service that these women had given to the Church.[42]

Once again, unfortunately, a pattern of misunderstanding, suspicion, and confrontation had been established within a congregation and in the relationship between many religious and members of the hierarchy. This divisiveness would continue to dominate the scene for the next 25 years.

Challenges facing men religious

Congregations of men religious were not immune to controversy during the years following the Council. Their points of difference with Vatican authorities, however, were most often less public than those of their sisters in religious life and, in general, centered on issues of priesthood. For example, the denial of a leadership role for brothers in clerical congregations was a concern for a number of groups. Brothers in congregations, such as the Franciscans, are usually ineligible to be elected to the office of General Superior or Provincial. In some groups, they are also denied the right to serve as a local superior, and, hence, are structurally powerless. With what justification? They lack the sacrament of holy orders.

The principle of jurisdiction is cited as the impediment to these men taking up a role of leadership within their congregations: a layperson cannot exercise authority over a cleric in matters relating to his priesthood. A brother has lay, not clerical, status. Unfortunately, this approach to authority makes eligibility for leadership within a religious congregation dependent upon ordination rather than religious consecration, a person's natural talents, and membership in the group.

In a second example, the Maryknoll community was discouraged from experimenting with new modes of association with its lay missionaries. This directive significantly weakened the ability of both groups to foster greater mutual partnership and to experiment with new forms of life together in community.

In still another example, early in 1990, officers of the National Board of the Conference of Major Superiors of Men met in Rome with representatives of the Vatican's Congregation for Divine Worship and the Discipline of the Sacraments. The leadership of CMSM had initiated the get-together to discuss a recent decision on the part of the Congregation that required men with a solemn vow of chastity to make also a promise of celibacy prior to ordination.

The outcome of the meeting was disappointing. Representatives of the Congregation pointed out repeatedly that issues pertaining to religious life fell under the competence of the Congregation for Institutes of Consecrated Life and Societies of Apostolic Life, whereas matters having to do with the sacrament of Holy Orders were the concern of the Congregation for Divine Worship and the Discipline of the Sacraments. The CMSM representatives left the meeting with the impression that the two Vatican congregations, though located only a few hundred yards from one another across the Piazza Pio XII, lacked an effective means to communicate with one another.

More to the point, the directive on the part of the Congregation for Divine Worship and the Discipline of the Sacraments that religious priests with a solemn vow of chastity also make a promise of celibacy demonstrated, at the very least, an insensitivity to the meaning and obligations of the vowed life. Priesthood had, once again, been given ascendancy over a man's commitment as a religious.

As if internal problems within congregations of men and some differences of opinion with the hierarchy were not enough of a tension, the problem of child sexual abuse among religious priests and brothers further eroded the morale of men religious. There is no denying that this tragic situation has not only harmed its victims, but has also had a corrosive effect on the image of male religious life in the States. While the frequency of incidences of child sexual abuse among religious priests and brothers appears about equivalent to its rate of occurrence among teachers, evidence exists today that these cases are, indeed, causing parents, and a number of men and women religious themselves, to discourage vocations to religious life.[43]

The context of change

Despite our good will and our strong desire to renew our mission, develop a spirituality that is charismatic and realistic, and form more life-giving Gospel-based communities, were we also somewhat naïve as we set out on the journey of renewal? Probably so. But then again, so were a number of others involved in the process. Boston College historian William Leonard, SJ, reminds us that the change brought about by Vatican II was extraordinary and unprecedented in our Church. "At no time in our history, perhaps," he wrote, "has so vast a cultural change come about in so short a time."[44]

Like most people, a number of us held fast to this erroneous belief: if change is necessary and explained carefully, we will be able to handle it! Many of us also failed to understand the difference between *change* and *the process of transformation.* The first occurs at a point in time, while the second takes place over time, giving people an opportunity to reorient themselves psychologically and spiritually to their changed situation.

What about mistakes? As we undertook the work of renewing our congregations, were we destined to make some? Without a doubt. In 1999, Doris Gottemoeller, RSM, a past President of the Leadership Conference of Women Religious and at the time President of the Sisters of Mercy of the Americas, suggested that what is truly amazing is that more mistakes were not made. The task of renewal was enormous, requiring as it did an examination and evaluation of every aspect of religious life and an appropriate revision of rules and constitutions, all in the space of about a dozen years. The success of the work depended also, in large measure, on the involvement and cooperation of approximately 180,000 women religious and 75,000 of their male counterparts.[45]

John Paul II expressed similar sentiments in a June 1998 *ad limina* address. The Pope remarked that: "religious life in the U.S. has been characterized by change and adaptation as called for by the Second Vatican Council and codified in canon law and other magisterial documents. This has not been an easy time," he went on to say, "since renewal of such complexity and far-reaching consequences involving so many people could not take place without much effort and strain."[46]

It is well to remember also that early attempts to renew U.S. religious life did not occur within a cultural or historical vacuum. Instead, they began to unfold during one of the most turbulent periods of social and political unrest in the country's recent history. An emerging counterculture was starting to divide the nation. Movements demanding greater civil, political, and sexual rights marked the 1960's in the States. So also did political assassinations, growing opposition to the war in Southeast Asia, and an increasing awareness of the exploitation and plight of women in society. Many people, feeling betrayed by the country's leaders, came to mistrust all forms of authority.

As we renovated the cloister in which we had lived for so many years, competing ideologies did battle with other values that had guided religious life. These ideologies included individualism, materialism, consumerism, and new understandings about sexuality and relationships, to name but a few. It was within all these rapidly changing circumstances that we began the work of adapting and renewing our congregations to the realities and needs of the Church and world. Despite whatever false starts may have occurred, this much became quickly apparent: the changes taking place were not going to be cosmetic. A full-scale revolution was underway.

Tensions increase

Tensions within a number of our religious congregations in the U.S. and between these groups and many of the country's bishops increased over the next ten years. Changing from religious habit to "secular" clothing, for example, or closing a longstanding congregational ministry often gave rise to painful disagreements.

Similar strain was evident on the national level. In 1975, for example, the first Women's Ordination Conference took place. The Vatican's Sacred Congregation for Religious asked the Leadership Conference of Women Religious, as the official representative of women religious in the States, to dissociate itself completely from the Conference and its goals. The Board of LCWR declined to do so. Four years later, during a pastoral visit to the United States, an obviously chagrined John Paul II heard Theresa Kane, RSM, LCWR president at the time, call on him to allow women to be ordained so as to affirm the Church's own teaching about the dignity of all persons.

The arrest of religious priests, sisters, and brothers protesting U.S. government policy at home and abroad, their growing involvement in ministries not common to their Institute, and the presence of some as members of national and state legislatures increased concern among Vatican officials that the majority of U.S. religious congregations were becoming too secularized and overly involved in social and political affairs. Consequently, in 1983, John Paul II wrote a letter to the American bishops directing them to undertake a study of religious life in the United States. The sharp drop in vocations to congregations was to be a special focus of the study.

Concern grew among a number of U.S. religious that an investigation was actually underway when the Congregation for Institutes of Consecrated Life and Societies of Apostolic Life released, at the same time as the Pope's letter, a document entitled *Essential Elements in Church Teaching on Religious Life.* Reaffirming as it did corporate apostolates, communities in which members of the same congregation lived together, and the wearing of a standard habit or religious garb, a number of women and men religious judged that the document repudiated many of the recent changes made in their way of life.

But the lowest point since Vatican II in the relationship between many religious congregations in the U.S. and the Vatican occurred late in 1984, during the presidential campaign. Geraldine Ferraro, a Catholic running for vice president on the Democratic ticket with Walter Mondale, was criticized by a number of bishops because of her pro-choice stand on abortion. Some observers read the bishops' repudiation of Ferraro as a signal to Catholics to vote against the Democratic candidates for president and vice president. In response, a group of Catholics took out a full-page ad in the October 7, 1984 issue of the *New York Times.* In it they stated that U.S. Catholics held a diversity of opinions on the question of abortion. Among the signers of the ad were three religious priests and brothers and twenty-six sisters.

Vatican authorities reacted quickly. The Superiors General of the signers' congregations received letters within a few weeks of the ad's appearance. They were instructed to have their members retract their statement or, if they refused to do so, face possible expulsion from their congregations. Working closely with CMSM and LCWR, those sisters, religious priests, and brothers involved, and their superiors, were able to examine the options available to them. Eventually, a compromise solution was worked out whereby most of the signers were able to issue statements of clarification. A few, however, left their congregations over the dispute.

Massive denial

In the early 1980's, Donna Markham, OP, a psychologist and consultant to the Pontifical Commission that studied U.S. religious life, characterized many religious in this country as being in a state of denial. Though aware of the large numbers who had departed from their groups and the lack of new recruits, they continued to resist the idea that their congregations might not have a future.

A 1986 *Wall Street Journal* article began to change all that. Entitled "Sisters in Need: U.S. Nuns Face Crisis as More Grow Older With Meager Benefits," the news story estimated a two billion dollar gap between the money available for the sisters' retirement and what was actually needed. As a consequence, some women religious were going on welfare, congregations were selling their motherhouses, and meatless meals, aimed at making ends meet, had become common. In the past, part of the income produced by the congregations' younger members helped support those who were aged and infirm. With many fewer entrants each year and a growing population of elderly sisters, the ability of most groups to continue this arrangement was seriously compromised.

In response to the crisis, the two religious conferences, along with the U.S. Bishops' Conference, set up the Tri-Conference Retirement Office, and the bishops authorized the first of a series of annual Church collections to create a retirement fund. Demonstrating an appreciation for what sisters, brothers, and religious priests had done for them, Catholics contributed so generously that the money gathered each year made this collection the single most successful appeal in the history of the Catholic Church in the U.S. The existence of the collection itself, however, also gave rise to at least one unfortunate consequence: in the minds of some Catholics, the appeal identified religious life as a dying enterprise.[47]

In yet another of many unexpected developments, on June 22, 1992, the Congregation for Institutes of Consecrated Life and Societies of Apostolic Life officially approved the formation of a new Council of U.S. Major Superiors of Women. Made up of members of the former Consortium Perfectae Caritatis, and representing 10,000 of the almost 100,000 women religious in the U.S. at the time, this new body was to have a standing equal to CMSM and LCWR. Unlike the other two Conferences, this new one would also have a direct episcopal liaison with Rome.

While the leadership of CMSM and LCWR were working to incorporate the new Council into presently existing structures, word came from Rome that a Synod on religious life was to be held in 1994. In light of the fact that most of the bishops participating in this gathering would not be members of religious congregations, U.S. brothers, sisters, and religious priests wondered just how much input into this meeting they might have. A number were also struck by the fact that many points raised in the working document of the soon to be held Synod bore striking resemblance to those made in the 1984 publication *Essential Elements.*

Echoes of the "Americanist" controversy

Since Vatican II, confrontation and misunderstanding obviously have not been strangers to the relationship between some Vatican authorities and a number of men and women religious in the U.S. As we have seen, plausible explanations abound to account for this state of affairs. The remnants of the now more than a century old Americanist controversy, however, may be another often overlooked factor contributing to the wariness found on both sides.

By the late 19th century, the Catholic Church in the States had grown in size, strength, and diversity, causing several of its leaders to stop and reflect on its distinct character and the direction in which it should be heading as the new century got underway.[48] This group—referred to as Americanists—argued that, with its size and power, the Catholic Church in the States was quite capable of governing itself in keeping with the New World's unique social, economic, and political environment. In their view, American democracy and the Church were not necessarily antagonistic. They also believed that with conservative European traditions on the wane, the Church could benefit from the experience of a truly pluralistic society.[49]

Not so, said those called Romanists. Looking to Rome for strong leadership, they held to an entirely different point of view. Convinced that the materialism and secular values of U.S. society were incompatible with the spiritual values of the Roman Catholic Church, the Romanists believed firmly that there was an inherent danger in attempting to reconcile the ideals of Catholicism with those of democracy.[50]

With convincing arguments on both sides, and great love of the Church evident, the two groups engaged in a spirited debate about the future character of the Church in the U.S. Unfortunately, this debate took place during a time when a number of radical, often violent, and usually anticlerical secret societies in Europe sought to dislocate governments, overturn churches, and generally revolutionize traditional society.

Concerned lest Catholics in the States be corrupted by secular philosophies and drawn into secret organizations, Romanist Church leaders moved to curtail Americanism. Catholics in the States were forbidden to join labor unions, even though the latter were devoid of the socialist and communist ideologies of their European counterparts. The leadership of the Americanist movement was also suppressed. Father Denis O'Connell, then Rector at the North American College in Rome, was replaced by Father William Henry O'Connell, a much more conservative clergyman who would soon afterwards be appointed Archbishop of Boston. A year later, Bishop John Keane, Rector of the Catholic University of America, was also removed in favor of a successor whose ideas were more in keeping with those of the Romanists.

Though at least one hundred years have passed since the height of the Americanist controversy, its effects can still be felt. They influence judgments made abroad about the attitudes of many U.S. Catholics, in general, and a number of women and men religious and their attempts to adapt and renew their way of life, in particular.[51]

Feminism

Throughout history[52] women have been treated in almost every culture as inferiors. Even those from affluent and privileged backgrounds commonly have been trivialized. Often enough, women were considered to be less than full persons. The imputed source of their inferiority? Their femaleness. Men, on the other hand, by virtue of being male, were characterized as superior, with a natural right to possess and control anyone or anything deemed inferior. When it came to women, the primary locus of male control was a woman's sexuality.

In recent years, feminism has reestablished a woman's right to "take back her sexuality,"[53] thus undermining any male claim to ownership and control. The reclaiming by women of their experience and their acceptance of it as equally normative to that of men has had a profound influence on the renewal of religious life in the U.S. Subsequent to Vatican II, many sisters' congregations established communities that reflected a vision of the Gospel community as a discipleship of equals. No longer were there to be "mothers" or "fathers" in the community, only sisters and brothers. Consequently, certain aspects of religious life—obscured during pre-conciliar times—had a chance to reemerge. Consecrated life was envisioned, more and more, as a voluntary community based on the principles of "from each according to her (his) ability and to each according to her (his) need."[54]

How would feminism view life in our Church? The following story will help us answer that question. During the Synod for Africa, a bishop in attendance suggested that women be made cardinals. The cardinalate, he pointed out, is, after all, a human invention and one that does not strictly require the sacrament of Holy Orders. Making women cardinals, the bishop reasoned, would be a rather ingenious way for the Church to allow them to share power without ordaining them priests. Reaction in the Synod hall split along two lines: chuckles from some, huffs of irritation from others. While the bishop's proposal went nowhere, its content illustrates the increasingly uneasy relationship between gender and authority in our Church.[55]

We all know that the Roman Catholic Church does not resemble a democracy. However, while in nations across the world, women occupy positions of significant leadership and authority, we don't find women in any of the top decision-making positions at the Vatican. Our Church as a whole has yet to sit down and listen thoughtfully to the experience of women and to accept it as equally valid to that of men. Women, for example, make up the majority of the members of religious congregations in this country. Despite that fact, in areas such as ministry, community, and spirituality, the experience of men has traditionally been taken as normative for all.[56] With what consequence? Women's experience has been diminished, ignored, or dismissed as irrelevant.

In any dialogue between our Church and women in the U.S., coming to a better understanding of the journey women religious have made since Vatican II will be an important part of the discussion. Among U.S. Catholics, no group has changed as visibly as they since the Council. And for good reason. Up until that time, their lives were characterized by anachronistic habits, cloistered convents, and a daily schedule suited more to an agrarian culture than to that in which the majority of them lived.[57]

During the years following Vatican II many changes took place. Theologian Sandra Schneiders, IHM, for example, reminds us that the class structure of choir and lay sister was abolished. Unilateral, top-down decision making was replaced by a structure in which all members were asked to take responsibility for determining the direction of the congregation's life and mission. On a more substantive level, the changes realized by congregations of women reflect an ecclesiology more in keeping with the ideals of the Council, but strikingly different from that embodied by the institutional Church, at least since the Reformation.[58]

What gave rise to these changes? The many dramatic developments taking place in society obviously played a role. So also did the reforms brought about by Vatican II, helping a number of women to understand the many ways in which they had been marginalized. The introduction of the vernacular into the liturgy, for example, brought to everyone's attention the fact that an almost exclusively male language was used to describe God.[59]

The question of women's ordination, high on the list of hopes expressed by many women in the Church, was addressed negatively by Pope John Paul II in his apostolic letter of May 22, 1994, "On Reserving Priestly Ordination to Men Alone" (*Ordinatio Sacerdotalis*). It left many Catholic women, as well as a number of men, angry and unhappy because they judged his argumentation to have been not only theologically flawed but also personally offensive. A further blow to women's aspirations along these lines was dealt by the Holy See on September 17, 2001 when it likewise forbade the establishment of programs that, in some way or other, looked to preparing women candidates for the diaconate. "In keeping with the constant ecclesiastical Magisterium," it stated, "the authentic promotion of woman in the Church opens other ample prospects of service and collaboration."

Prophetic Christian feminism gives us another insight into the Gospel message. By emphasizing interdependence in relationships, Christian feminism fosters dialogue and strikes a welcome balance between self-sacrifice for the good of others and self-assertion for the good of self and society. Resolving the tension between dependence and a wholesome autonomy, however, is not just a challenge for women, but one we all must face.

Despite Christian feminism's positive contribution to the renewal of religious life, it too fell victim to the atmosphere of suspicion and mistrust that marked so many encounters between members of religious congregations and Church authorities during the years since the Council.

Collaboration between the religious conferences, and with the Bishops' Conference

Tensions between some members of the two religious conferences also arose from time to time. A number of women religious resented being labeled as "radical feminists" by some bishops, men religious, and lay men and women whenever they took a stand on behalf of women and their rights in society and Church. Likewise, many of their ordained brothers in consecrated life took exception when blamed for the sins of clericalism throughout the centuries.

Despite these tensions, and although many of their concerns varied, the leadership of CMSM and LCWR grew ever more collaborative over time. Joint assemblies were held periodically. Since 1989, representatives of both conferences annually travel to Rome as one delegation to meet with representatives of the Congregation for Religious and Secular Institutes and several other Vatican offices. These yearly get-togethers foster a spirit of dialogue and help correct misconceptions on both sides.

Similarly, lines of communication between CMSM and LCWR and the U.S. Bishops' Conference were strengthened when the Tri-Conference Commission on Religious Life and Ministry was formed. Coming to life as a result of *Mutuae Relationes,* a document addressing the relationship between the hierarchy and religious congregations, the Commission was made up of representatives from the three conferences. During its early years, this group met regularly so as to address topics of significant concern for religious, and to keep open lines of communication among the larger bodies they represented. Though known primarily because of its involvement with the annual collection for retired religious, the Tri-Conference Commission has the potential to render a more important service, i.e., fostering ongoing dialogue between men and women religious and the bishops of the country.

Difficult decisions

As U.S. religious life moved toward the third millennium, this much was apparent: if asked about the meaning and purpose of consecrated life, many of us—brothers, religious priests, and sisters—had no clear nor commonly held answer. Religious life's lack of identity had serious consequences for everything from encouraging vocations to fostering a contemporary understanding of the evangelical counsels of chastity, obedience, and poverty.

Wittberg points out that, despite all the good will on the part of the vast majority of us, some of the decisions we made during the process of renewal led ultimately to a self-defeating way of operating.[60] Some mission statements developed by congregations were so vague and general that they managed to include all the various interests found among the group members. But the lack of a deeply shared common vision made it quite difficult to make congregational decisions, especially in terms of long-range planning. With what consequences? The near impossibility of sustaining corporate commitments.

Also, whenever we chose to classify spirituality as a private concern, work as an individual project, and the personal growth of our membership as more important than the valid needs of the group, we helped compromise any possible future that our congregations might have. Cultural conformity ended up taking precedence over prophetic challenge.[61]

As if to give evidence to support this last contention, David Nygren, CM, and Miriam Ukeritis, CSJ, an organizational and a clinical psychologist respectively, conducted a wide ranging study of women and men in religious orders in the U.S. Called the FORUS study (Future of Religious Life in the United States), it involved 9,999 U.S. sisters, religious priests, and brothers. The investigation's final report included this sobering judgment: *"Without significant change, religious life in the United States will continue to decline, and, more important, those who need the help of these orders will not be cared for."*[62] The findings of this piece of research caused many U.S. men and women religious to pause and look seriously at the outcome of 30 years of renewal in U.S. religious life. They began to realize that the time had come for some difficult decisions.

31

Vita Consecrata

Future analysts may judge the 1994 Synod on consecrated life to be a significant turning point in the efforts of men and women religious in the States to revitalize their way of living out the Gospel. Many sisters, religious priests, and brothers, as they prepared for the Synod, were forced to take a hard look at the results of their efforts to adapt and renew religious life in the U.S.

More importantly, however, *Vita Consecrata*—the Apostolic Exhortation that was the fruit of the Synod—took some long over-due steps toward redefining the identity of religious life for the present age. Before discussing the special value of consecrated life, however, Pope John Paul II first pointed out that each of the fundamental states of life within our Church—lay, ordained ministry, and consecrated life—expresses one or another aspect of the mystery of Christ. Lay men and women take on responsibility for the mission of insuring that the Gospel message is proclaimed in the temporal sphere. Bishops are entrusted with the task of guiding the People of God by proclaiming the Word, administering the sacraments, and using their authority to promote communion within the Church.[63]

Religious life, which mirrors Christ's own way of life, has, in the Pope's words, a certain excellence[64] or pre-eminence in its ability to carry out the task of showing forth the Church's holiness. It proclaims and, in a way, anticipates a future age when the reign of God will be achieved, and is a more complete expression of the Church's purpose: the sanctification of humanity.[65]

John Paul II also observed that, similar to other states of life, within religious life there are a number of different but complementary paths. Some of us devote ourselves to contemplation; we image in a special way Christ on the mountain. In contrast, those of us in the active life witness to Christ proclaiming the reign of God to the multitudes.[66]

The text of *Vita Consecrata* makes an important distinction between Church structures and the lived experience of the People of God. Within the structure of the Church, there are only two states of life: the lay and the clerical. However, within the Church's lived experience, there are three: the lay, clerical, and religious states. Building upon these distinctions, religious life was able to take another step toward clarifying its identity and its place in our Church. With that task underway, and almost a half-century of experimentation behind us, many of us who made up U.S. religious life found ourselves in a more hopeful position to re-imagine our way of life for a new millennium. The next few chapters of this book suggest a plan of action for accomplishing that task. Before moving on, however, let's first answer this pressing question about religious life in our country and its future: Do you and I really believe that it has one?

Reflection questions

1. Take some time to look at the history of renewal in your own congregation, institute, or province.
   * Beginning in 1950, trace the process of adaptation and revitalization that took place.
   * Identify those moments marked by boldness and risk-taking that were guided by the Spirit.
   * What pitfalls did your group also fail to avoid?
   * If you were to begin again and undertake the process of revitalizing your congregation, institute, or province a second time, just what might you do, and what mistakes might you avoid making?

Suggested process for use with small groups

1. Ask each group member to take 60 minutes of quiet reflective time to consider prayerfully the above questions. Ask each person to write out the fruit of his/her reflection and prayer.
2. After one hour, assemble in small groups of no more than eight persons each. These units may be made up, for example, of the members of a local community of six persons or two different smaller communities of three or four persons each that have come together for the occasion. Prior to the groups coming together, appoint a leader for each. The leader's role is to get the sharing started by asking each member to identify the significant moments in his or her congregation or province's history in the U.S. over the past half-century.
3. The group can appoint a secretary, if desired, to organize a written summary of the main points of its exchange.

Notes

[1] Center for the Applied Research on the Apostolate (CARA report, 2000). See also Gustav Niebuhr, "Recruiting Pitch: Monastic Life, for 3 Days," *New York Times* HTTP://WWW.NYTIMES.COM/2001/01/13/NATIONAL/13MONK.HTML.
[2] Patricia Wittberg, *The Rise and Fall of Catholic Religious Orders*, 1.
[3] Ravi Perumani, "Catholic Nuns are Aging," *Hindustan Today* (October 1997) HTTP://WWW.HVK.ORG/HVK/ARTICLES/0997/0080.HTML.
[4] Ibid.
[5] Arthur Jones, "Nuns Renew Vows," *National Catholic Reporter* 35:18 (March 5, 1999), 11-18.
[6] Source, National Religious Retirement Office.
[7] Jan Kerkhofs, SJ, "Europe needs therapy," *The Tablet* (July 23, 1999) HTTP://WWW.THETABLET.CO.UK.
[8] Source, HTTP://WWW.TASC.AC.UK/CC/%20/STATS/STX08.HTM.
[9] Dilanni, "Religious Life: Directions for a Future," 343.
[10] Source, Brother Charles J. Jackson, SJ, Jesuit Curia, Rome, Italy.
[11] Dilanni, "Vocations: New Signs of the Times," 746.

[12] Ibid., 747.

[13] Ibid.

[14] Quoted in Brian John Sweeney, FMS, *The Patrimony of an Institute and the Code of Canon Law: A Study of Canon 578* (Rome: Dissertatio ad Lauream in Facultate Juris Canonici Apud Pontificiam Universitatem S. Thomae in Urbe, 1995), 17.

[15] Quoted in Mary L. Schneider, "The Transformation of American Women Religious: The Sister Formation Conference as a Catalyst for Change, 1954-1964," *Cushwa Center Working Paper Series* 17:1 (Spring 1986), University of Notre Dame, 6-7.

[16] Lora Ann Quinonez and Mary Daniel Turner, *The Transformation of American Catholic Sisters* (Philadelphia, PA: Temple University Press, 1992), 6.

[17] Ibid.

[18] Ibid., 94-95.

[19] Prior to Vatican II, and often enough during the years to follow, the temporal and spiritual health of an apostolic congregation was determined by its number of novices and the rate of expansion of its institutional network, such as schools or hospitals.

[20] Fleming, "Understanding a Theology of Religious Life," 32-49.

[21] Ibid.

[22] Edward Stourton, *Absolute Truth: The Catholic Church Today* (London: Penguin Books, 1998), 205.

[23] John L. Allen, Jr., "The Vatican's Enforcer," *National Catholic Reporter* 35:24 (April 16, 1999), 17-18.

[24] Giuseppe Alberigo and Jean-Pierre Jossua, and Joseph A. Komonchak, eds., *Reception of Vatican II* (Washington, DC: The Catholic University of America, 1988).

[25] Austin Flannery, OP, ed., *The Basic Sixteen Documents: Vatican Council II* (Northport, NY: Costello Publishing Company, 1996), 59-60.

[26] Ibid., 67.

[27] Sweeney, *The Patrimony of an Institute in the Code of Canon Law,* 24.

[28] Ibid.

[29] Sean O'Riordan, "Religious Life in a Time of Turbulence," *Religious Life Review* 32:3 (May/June 1993) 157.

[30] Quoted in Peter E. Fink, SJ, "Religious Obedience and the Holy Spirit," *Review for Religious* 30:1 (January/February 1971) 64-79.

[31] Wittberg, *The Rise and Fall of Catholic Religious Orders,* 243.

[32] Flannery, *The Basic Sixteen Documents: Vatican Council II,* 392.

[33] Marist Brothers Archives, *Proceedings of the 16th General Chapter: 1967-1968.*

[34] *Ecclesiae Sanctae II,* 1.

[35] Ibid.

[36] Ibid., 6.

[37] Sweeney, *The Patrimony of an Institute in the Code of Canon Law,* 116.

[38] *Evangelica Testificatio,* 51.

[39] Maria Augusta Neal, SNDdeN, *Catholic Sisters in Transition: From the 1960's to the 1980's* (Wilmington, DE: Michael Glazier, 1984).

[40] Mark S. Massa, *Catholics and American Culture: Fulton Sheen, Dorothy Day, and*

the Notre Dame Football Team (New York, NY: The Crossroad Publishing Company, 1999), 172.

[41] Ibid., 175.

[42] Carroll Stuhlmueller, "Biblical Observations on the Decline of Vocations to Religious Life," in Laurie Felknor, ed., *The Crisis in Religious Vocations: An Inside View* (Mahwah, NJ: Paulist, Press, 1989), 163.

[43] Stephen J. Rossetti, *A Tragic Grace: The Catholic Church and Child Sexual Abuse* (Collegeville, MN: Liturgical Press, 1996).

[44] Cited in Thomas H. O'Connor's *Boston Catholics: A History of the Church and its People* (Boston, MA: Northeastern University Press, 1998), 265.

[45] Doris Gottemoeller, RSM, "Religious Life in Crisis," *Origins* 28:36 (February 25, 1999), 634-638.

[46] *Origins 28:*10 (August 13, 1998), 170.

[47] Helen Maher Garvey, BVM. "Almost any group?" In *Salt Online* http://www.bvmcong.org/salt/salt/Fall1999/garvey.htm.

[48] O'Connor, *Boston Catholics,* 183.

[49] Ibid., 183-184.

[50] Ibid., 184-185.

[51] Chester Gillis, *Roman Catholicism in America* (New York, NY: Columbia University Press, 1999), 66.

[52] Staff of the Economist, "Trafficking in Women: In the shadows," *The Economist* 356:8185 (August 26, 2000), 18-19.

[53] Sandra Schneiders, *With Oil in Their Lamps: Faith, Feminism, and the Future* (Mahwah, NJ: Paulist Press, 2000), 7-12.

[54] Ibid., 69.

[55] Robert Mickens, "The Vatican: it's still a man's world," in *Priests and People* 14:8,9 (August/September 2000), http://www.thetablet.com/priestsandpeople.co.uk/ppcaug00.htm.

[56] Brian O'Leary, SJ, "Developments in Christian Spirituality Since Vatican II," *Religious Life Review* 38:197 (July/August 1999), 212-228.

[57] Schneiders, *With Oil in Their Lamps,* 67.

[58] Ibid., 67-68.

[59] Ibid., 57.

[60] Wittberg, *The Rise and Fall of Catholic Religious Orders,* 256.

[61] David Nygren and Miriam Ukeritis, *The Future of Religious Orders in the United States: Transformation and Commitment* (Westport, CT: Praeger, 1993), 244-246.

[62] Ibid., 257.

[63] *Post-Synodal Apostolic Exhortation Vita Consecrata* http://www.vatican.va/holy_father/john_Yii_exh_25031996_vita-conscrata_en.html, 16.

[64] Ibid.

[65] Ibid.

[66] Ibid., 17.

REVITALIZATION: READING THE TEA LEAVES

Let's stop for a moment and consider this fundamental question: "Do you and I believe that a revitalization of U.S. religious life is possible today?" That's right, despite all the losses of the past 40 or so years, are we convinced that a rebirth of consecrated life in this country is in the offing? The energy we are willing to spend and the risks we are prepared to take will all be determined by our answer to that basic question. To aid us in putting together our response, let's look at the facts that we have on hand.

Over the last half-century we have witnessed the dismantling of consecrated life as we once knew it. We have also lived through the steady erosion of ways of thinking and systems of belief that once served us well as men and women religious. Early in this process, for example, a number of us reexamined and eventually judged as no longer useful some customs and practices that had gone unquestioned in our congregations for decades. We also came to see that many of our ways of living together and the work we had undertaken could no longer handle the important new challenges we faced.[1]

As problems grew, how did we respond? Initially, by applying all the standard remedies. Some of us suggested that a recommitment on the part of our congregations to doing what we had always done well would do the trick. Others among us championed the renewal of individuals. "Change hearts and you will revitalize the group," we said. Still others argued for a break with the past. Much of what the community believed, we pointed out, was archaic, bound in the trappings and language of a bygone age. As we can see in retrospect, the usual problem-solving techniques did not work.

So, what happened? A sense of crisis set in as traditional structures of authority and new methods for arriving at decisions within the community became confused. Over time, a number of our groups appeared to lose their direction and sense of purpose. The service they rendered to the Church became haphazard, and appeared aimless. Withdrawals from our congregations increased. The number of new recruits dropped off dramatically. Long-standing works were abandoned. "Business as usual" came to a stop. Unanswered questions about our function and purpose began to accumulate. Doubts about the future grew. Some of us began to wonder if we had any future at all.[2]

How can we make some sense of this sequence of events? Perhaps by admitting, first of all, that God can still be found in the midst of the current crisis in U.S. religious life. And then, by accepting the fact that the tools of social science, while offering some insight, will always be found wanting when applied to events that must be seen through the eyes of faith.

Jesus came proclaiming the reign of God, its imminence, and our need to prepare for it. Religious life ought to be the Church's memory of this central truth of our faith. Marianist brother Stephen Glodek brings this point home using a story from the tradition of the Hasidim.[3] The tale is about the great Rabbi Naptali. Every evening after the sun went down, he had the custom of walking through town and then into its outskirts. His daily constitutional gave him time to reflect, and also helped him keep up with the comings and goings of his neighbors.

Wealthy landowners in this town had the custom of hiring watchmen to guard the perimeters of their property at night. One evening after dark, the rabbi came across one of these watchmen and asked him for the name of his employer. A familiar one was given in answer.

To the surprise of the rabbi, the watchman next asked him about his employer. The question hit the clergyman squarely in the heart, stopping him in his tracks. Wasn't it obvious to the watchman and indeed to all the world, the rabbi wondered, that he worked for the Master of the Universe? Unsure of himself now, the rabbi delayed giving an answer, and instead walked with the watchman along the grounds of the rich man's estate. Eventually, the rabbi spoke. "I'm sorry to say," he admitted, "that I am not sure that I really work for anyone. You see, I am the rabbi in this town."

After a long, silent walk, the rabbi asked the watchman, "Will you come and work for me?"

"Of course, I would be delighted to," responded the watchman, "What would my duties entail?"

The rabbi replied, "Oh, there would be just one thing that you would always do. Remind me for whom I work, in whose employ I am, and why I am here. Just remind me—that's all."

In light of our almost 40 years of efforts aimed at renewing U.S. religious life, we could very well believe that we are the rabbi in this tale, ever in need of being reminded for whom we work. However, as men and women religious, our place is among those who watch. We are called to live in darkness on the perimeter and to remind our Church constantly about its true identity.[4]

What is needed today to fulfill this important role? Credibility in the eyes of the People of God. In the past we measured the presence of this virtue by the size of our memberships, the reputation of our institutions, and the prestige in which our Church and congregations were held. How times have changed! Today we are better off using Jesus' criteria for measuring credibility. Do we live as if the Spirit of the Lord is upon us? Are we bringing *Good News* to the poor? Proclaiming release to captives? Freeing the oppressed? Giving sight to the blind? Announcing the favor of the Lord?[5]

Effective communication also fosters credibility. In recent years, unfortunately, we have at times been less than successful in this area. For example, ask yourself this question: "When it comes to renewal, who understands what we as religious are talking about?" Throughout the last four decades of change and upheaval in consecrated life, some of us appear to have been talking to ourselves more than to anyone else.[6] The time has come to include more fully the entire People of God in our conversation about renewal.

Delivering the message

Throughout history, those who have followed Jesus radically have delivered his message about God's reign and its immanence in a number of different and novel ways. Not surprising. After all, as religious aren't we charged with responsibility for telling the story of God's deeds by means of personal example and in a language that is easily understood?[7]

The early disciples spoke about the importance of prayer and reflection. While these practices were not unknown in pre-Christian communities such as the Essenes, both flourished in the cenobitic and monastic traditions. Mary of Egypt and Anthony, in particular, learned the language of the desert, and Benedict and Scholastica made the desert story fruitful in still another way by reminding us that Jesus' story is about community.[8]

Over time, many communities lost sight of Jesus' message, and gave priority, instead, to structures and customs. They also focused more and more on wealth, power, and prestige. Having strayed from their founding purpose, some eventually fell into decline.

Church historian John Padberg, SJ, points out that during the past 450 years, religious life in the western Church passed through three major periods of upheaval. The first began with the Protestant Reformation. The second came to life around the time of the French Revolution, and our most recent period of turmoil got under way during the years following Vatican II.[9]

At the time of the Protestant Reformation, consecrated life was suffering from a credibility problem. So bad had its reputation become, that more than once the Holy See received a proposal that all but four orders of men and most orders of women be suppressed.[10] The Church's calls for the reform of consecrated life went largely unheeded.

Recurring patterns of decline, however, cannot fully explain the evolution of consecrated life over the centuries. How account for the apparent cyclical pattern of growth and falling off— a blueprint that mirrors the death and resurrection of Jesus— observed throughout the history of religious life? After all, in the midst of the upheaval set in motion by Martin Luther and others, a Catholic Reformation eventually took root and spread. New religious congregations sprang up, grew in numbers, and flourished. Some older orders took themselves in hand, made necessary changes, and prospered once more.

Let's admit it: God is with us in powerful ways during our days of decline. This very same God also has the knack of raising up in our Church women and men who can provide us, when needed, with new and prophetic images of consecrated life.

41

God did just that with Francis and Clare. They drew the poor once again to the attention of a community that had forgotten them. The followers of Ignatius and Dominic worked hard, too, to insure that the story of Jesus made sense intellectually, particularly when confronted with competing stories.[11] In retrospect, we can see that Ignatius and Dominic, as well as Francis and Clare, offered to their contemporaries a new model of religious life, one better suited to the times in which they lived.

In the 19th century, Marcellin Champagnat,[12] following the tradition of Jean Baptiste de La Salle, reminded our Church once again that the story of Jesus needed to be shared with poor young people. Likewise, in post-industrial society, Catherine McAuley, Katharine Drexel, and others reminded all of us that the story of Jesus is to be told most especially to the least among us.[13] Consequently, the congregations they and others formed proclaim the reign of God in still another way.

Combining elements of both the monastic and mendicant traditions, this new generation of founders and foundresses set out to address some of the urgent human needs left in the wake of the Industrial Revolution. Education and health care became their primary apostolates.

However, true to form, many of us who are members of these groups eventually forgot our primary purpose: to proclaim God's reign and its immanence. The recent almost four decades of upheaval and steady congregational decline in the U.S. have reminded us in part about the foundation upon which our life must be built.

An answer to our question

Knowledge of religious life's history encourages us to have a cautious optimism and to answer "yes" to our question: "Do we believe that a revitalization of religious life in the U.S. is possible today?" After all, our way of life has been renewed before. However, the challenges we face are far from simple. As mentioned in the *Introduction* to this book, at least three likely outcomes are possible for congregations existing in the States today: extinction, minimal survival, and rebirth.

Extinction obviously occurs when a congregation disappears from the scene. All of its members withdraw or eventually die off. Today, rather than search for a new identity, some men and women religious have concluded that their group has, in fact, finished its mission in our Church and world and is currently in the process of dying.

Their decision is not without precedent. Sixty-four percent of religious orders of men founded before 1800 no longer exist. We can reasonably expect, therefore, that some present day congregations will not survive the transition in which religious life finds itself at the moment.[14]

One caution, however: while we must admit that religious orders are founded, flourish, and eventually die as part of a natural process of evolution, we also need to be careful not to make decisions about our congregations that will contribute to their death. Why? Because they do not belong to those of us who make up their memberships. They belong, instead, to the People of God. In joining a religious order, one takes on a special responsibility for stewarding its charism, spirituality, and mission. One cannot, however, claim the group itself as one's private property. Decisions about ending its life need to be made in consultation with the wider Church community.

Also, some current congregations will move in the direction of minimal survival. Examining the membership patterns of groups founded before the French Revolution, we find that most entered into a period lasting several centuries during which the number of sisters, priests, or brothers who constituted the congregation was very small in comparison to its time of peak membership.[15] But such an outcome should not always be interpreted as a sign of diminishment. The Carthusians have followed this pattern, yet their spiritual impact continues to far exceed the group's numerical strength.

A small percentage of religious orders, however, generally survive a critical time of transition and enter into a period of revitalization. These groups are marked by three distinct characteristics: one, *a transforming response to the signs of the times;* two, *a reappropriation of the founding charism;* three, *a profound renewal of the members' lives of faith, spirituality, and centeredness in Christ.*[16]

Recent developments[17]

When discussing recent efforts on behalf of renewal among religious congregations in the United States, Dominican Paul Philibert borrows a model from H. Richard Niebuhr. The latter proposed three major poles that represent either a conflict between Christ and culture (radical Christianity), a surrender of Christian tradition to culture (cultural Christianity), or the transformation of culture by Christian tradition (the transformative model).

Using Niebuhr's framework, Philibert speaks about a radical, a cultural, and a transformative vision of religious life. In explaining the first, or radical, vision of consecrated life, he points out that there are some people in the U.S. today who believe that a return to pre-conciliar attitudes and institutions is the most appropriate response to the last 40 years of renewal.

Radical vision of religious life

Prior to Vatican II, the relationship between the Catholic Church and the country's culture was often escapist and defensive. Living in a religious ghetto, many Catholics saw themselves as outsiders in American culture. Their job was to protect themselves from the immoral influences found in their society. Within this worldview, those who wished to live Christianity in a radical way had no choice but to separate themselves from the corrupting culture of the world.

After all, that world had been spoiled by the fall of Adam. Pessimistic about human achievements, this radical model of Christianity was characterized by a passion for order and uniformity achieved through authority, law, and predictable expressions of tradition. Religious life was defined by the norms and obligations of cloister, rule, and religious habit. Unquestioning obedience was its fundamental virtue. Is it any wonder, then, that John XXIII's daring decision to call a Church Council and welcome the process of renewal shook the whole Church to its foundations?

Within the dynamics of radical consecrated life, some religious superiors tended to treat those in their charge like children, regardless of their age, experience, or intellect. With what consequence? The moral experience of those with whom they shared religious life was infantilized. Vatican II, with its insistence on the moral autonomy of Christians, the participation of all in public life, and the responsibility to read the signs of the times, changed all that forever.

Cultural vision of religious life

The years just after the Council gave rise to what Niebuhr characterized as "cultural Christianity." Those espousing this point of view saw little division between gospel and culture. They were, by nature, optimists and judged whatever the culture produced that was fine, exciting, or promising to be an apt expression of grace.

An instinct for relevance was at the heart of cultural Christianity. It emerged in the U.S. about the same time that young Americans started to celebrate the alternate wisdom they were finding in drugs, meditation, New Age ideas, and Eastern philosophy.

Men and women religious who adopted this cultural model came to see pre-conciliar attitudes and institutions as problematic. A faithful renewal of their way of life, therefore, had to be revolutionary. Consequently, they worked to reduce the separation between their religious culture and the general culture, and to foster among their congregations' members an almost universal participation in the processes of government and society.

Philibert makes special mention of two important and positive aspects of this cultural model as it applies to consecrated life. First of all, he points out that during this period many religious were intensely involved in work for justice. Of particular note was their awareness that justice is concerned with the reformation of the social order.

Second, he points out that creative leadership was particularly evident among the members of congregations of women religious. They were far more responsive to the Council's call for renewal than were their male counterparts. Philibert speculates that this difference, in part, had to do with the investment that many men who were clerics made in their status as priests and their fuller identification with the hierarchy.

46

Today, however, the cultural model appears to have run its course. Vocations are slim, so the model is failing to replicate itself. A discrepancy between the cultural experience of today's young adults and the ecclesial passions of religious who came of age at the time of Vatican II is also evident.

The war stories of those of us who lived out part of our religious life prior to Vatican II are both unintelligible and uninteresting to those among our membership born 15 years after the Council's closing session. In addition, we can see, in retrospect, that some of the decisions we made to cast off practices that were part of radical religious life (retreat days, institutional commitments, liturgical observances) were often more of a reaction to the authoritarianism of the period than anything else.

Transformative vision of religious life

Niebuhr's transformative model can help us understand some recent developments in a number of religious communities. Being neither pessimistic nor optimistic, this model is realistic in that it recognizes the problems of an unconverted world. Within the model, there is neither a gap nor a concordance between gospel and culture, but rather a critical engagement of culture by the gospel. Whereas radical religious fled the world, and cultural religious embraced it, transformative religious want to redefine that very same world. For them, the world and the gospel are in dialogue: the world as incarnation, the gospel as inspiration.

Holiness takes on different expressions in each of these models. The radical religious achieved holiness by following the rule and submitting to obedience, while immersion in ordinary life events spelled holiness for the cultural religious. Transformative holiness has an entirely different face. Women and men religious live it out when they become bearers of God's Spirit. Their religious culture provides them with the means to do so: dynamic silence, sensitivity to the interior word through study and recollection, spiritual hospitality, and spiritual work. This type of holiness, according to Philibert, allows the gospel to illumine and stabilize our lives in such a way that it can be fruitful in genuine human community and in the world.

Application of the transformative model

Commitment mechanisms such as separation, cloister, and distinct dress have been a source of conflict between—for lack of better terms—traditional and progressive outlooks during postconciliar renewal. For example, whereas radical religious accepted community as an institutional fact to be taken for granted, cultural religious defined it as an elective option, and sometimes opted out. Transformative religious, in contrast, seek a middle ground: in choosing to live the common life, they also choose to live and share in faith the rule and constitutions of their group. Consequently, their commitment to one another makes them genuinely accountable to the group.

Prayer also takes on a different form within each of the three models. For radical religious, prayer is fundamentally institutional. They recite the *Liturgy of the Hours* and the devotional formulas prescribed by their congregation's *Rule of Life.*

In contrast, prayer tends to be functional for cultural religious. They decide what is spiritually useful and inspiring—and "feels right"—for themselves.

Transformative religious have still another experience of prayer. For them, its style tends toward the contemplative and is more holistic than the prayer experience of either the radical or cultural religious. While there is a new appreciation for the *Lit-*

urgy of the Hours among transformative religious, especially in light of more satisfying current renditions of Church psalms and chants, silence has also become an important part of their community prayer.

Applications of this model can be made to the evangelical counsels, ecclesiology, and a number of other areas. Philibert advocates the use of this model to advance the work of renewing and adapting consecrated life among religious in the U.S. He challenges us to reinvest religious community living with robust expressions of the transcendent and the immanent, to attend to the dynamic transitions inaugurated by Vatican II, and to remember other key challenges that arose from that Council: ecumenism, inculturation, and cultural creativity.

Neo-radical religious

Philibert also makes a helpful distinction between neo-radical and transformative religious. These two groups, though quite different, are often confused with one another. Those in the first are actually trying to restore what existed in the past. However, they often appear to get lost in the paraphernalia of their alternative world and become defensive about their traditional approach to consecrated life.

Transformative religious, in contrast, while as concerned about identity, community, spirituality, and mission as their neo-radical brothers and sisters, take a middle position. They are knowledgeable about their religious tradition, and familiar with the world. At the same time, they judge both these realities in light of their experience of the Spirit in a living community of prayer, ministry, and communion. Their challenge? To realize that the signs of our times demand a transformative vision of religious life and to find ways to describe what it can and should look like.

Today, as we struggle to renew and adapt our congregations, we also do well to remember the context in which we carry out this work. As mentioned earlier, throughout its history religious life has passed through several major eras: the ages of the Desert, Monasticism, the rise of the Mendicants, and so forth. When revitalization takes place midway during one of these eras, it takes on the characteristics of a reform, with reappropriation of the founding charism playing a more central role.[18]

However, contemporary U.S. religious life is working toward a rebirth during an era when a paradigmatic shift of enormous consequence is taking place. The dominant image of religious life itself is changing. *Throughout such a period, congregations that move in the direction of vitality typically take on many of the characteristics of the new and emerging image of consecrated life. A transforming response to the signs of the times is also central to this process.*[19] Included among those signs today are these two: (1) the keen interest that young people have in the radical possibility of adults trying to live together in community so as to witness to reconciliation and peace,[20] and (2) the hunger of these adults for a spirituality that makes room for the presence of God in their lives and the presence of life in their spirituality and prayer.

Reflection Question

Using the format set out at the end of Chapter I, please spend some time reflecting on the following question:

1. What is your response to this question: "Do you believe that a revitalization of U.S. religious life is possible today?" If you are cautiously optimistic about the future of consecrated life in the States, what is the source of your opti-

mism? If your answer to the question is "no," on what facts or intuitions do you base your response?

Notes

[1] Cada, et. al., *Shaping the Coming Age of Religious Life*, 59.
[2] Ibid., 58-59.
[3] Stephen Glodek, "Is anyone listening to us?" *Presidential Address,* The Conference of Major Superiors of Men (New Orleans, LA: CMSM, August 12, 2000) http://www.cmsm.org/News/Assembly%202000/postassembly.htm.
[4] Ibid.
[5] Ibid.
[6] Ibid.
[7] Ibid.
[8] Ibid.
[9] Padberg, "The Contexts of Comings and Goings," 20 B21.
[10] Ibid.
[11] Glodek, *Presidential Address.*
[12] Seán D. Sammon, FMS, *A Heart that Knew No Bounds: The Life and Mission of Saint Marcellin Champagnat* (Staten Island, NY: Alba House, 2000).
[13] Glodek, *Presidential Address.*
[14] Cada et al., *Shaping the Coming Age of Religious Life,* 59.
[15] Ibid.
[16] Ibid., 60.
[17] Beginning with this section of the chapter and for its remainder, the author is indebted to the work of Paul Philibert, OP, "Toward a Transformative Model of Religious Life," 9-14.
[18] Ibid.
[19] Ibid.
[20] Osiek, "A woman stands at Mount Nebo."

Chapter III

A
FORK
IN THE
ROAD

Within weeks of Joseph Bernardin's death from cancer in November 1996, his physician Ellen Gaynor, OP, had this to say about her relationship with the Cardinal: "I found early on that I was strongly drawn to him." But the doctor, who attended the late Archbishop of Chicago during his final illness, faced a dilemma as she struggled to put her finger on just what it was that drew her so quickly to Bernardin. Was it his kind and gentle nature, sharp mind, or quick wit that she found so attractive? Eventually, Gaynor realized that some entirely different qualities caused the Cardinal to stand out from many of her other patients: his simplicity, courage, and great faith. "After all," she said, "he asked only that I be honest with him."

Gaynor's last encounter with Joseph Bernardin says it all: "When I saw him on the Friday before his death, I told him that he would die before Christmas. He said simply, 'I am ready.' I promised him also that I would tell him when he was very close to death, and when I saw him three days later, there had been rapid deterioration. So, I said to him, 'You are very close, you will die this week. Are you OK with this?' To which he replied, 'If it must be, I am ready.'" Inner peace such as that displayed by

Joseph Bernardin does not just happen; it has to be nurtured over a lifetime.

The Cardinal's life and death remind us that personal witness can still be a powerful tool for promoting the message of Jesus. Consider the extraordinary news coverage during the days preceding and following his death, and the positive reactions to the publication of his memoir, *The Gift of Peace,* as well as the many books about the Cardinal's life and ministry that appeared in its wake. Delivering the eulogy at Bernardin's funeral, friend and confidant Monsignor Ken Velo described the Cardinal's life as a remarkable human and spiritual adventure. Those listening to him could only agree.

Many religious in the U.S. today share Joseph Bernardin's hopes and dreams, and his concern for our Church and world. The lives of some of us, however, differ from his in one very significant way. The late Cardinal's identity as a Church minister was clear and apparent; often ours is not. Whereas many contemporary American men and women religious are invisible, everyone knew that Joseph Bernardin was, first and foremost, a priest.

Crisis of identity

Our lack of visibility is but one obstacle to overcome if we are to revitalize consecrated life and its mission for the century just beginning. We will also need to explain, to ourselves and everyone else, just what it is that makes our lives as religious different from any other equally valid way of living out Jesus' message. Joseph Bernardin's *identity* was clear. For ours to be, too, we must decide what it means today to be a sister, religious priest, or brother.

What do we mean by the word, *identity*? On a personal

level, it is that feeling of knowing who we are and where we are going in life. Organizational or institutional identity is much the same. When asked what they stand for, groups with a strong identity have a ready and compelling answer to give. Just as personal identity helps distinguish you and me from one another and makes us unique, a religious congregation's identity helps its members answer these two questions: "Who are we?" and "What do we stand for?"

In the past, the identity of women and men religious in the U.S. was clear, at least to Roman Catholics. Forty years ago, if you mentioned to any Catholic school child the term "Sister," you got a look of instant recognition. Young people might not have known all the details of religious life, but at least they could identify those of us who lived it. We were people set apart. Having pledged ourselves to live the evangelical counsels more intensely, we had also given up several things that most people could expect to have: a spouse, money and some control over it, a degree of freedom in making certain decisions.

Today, however, we find a very different reality: external elements that once made the identity of our way of life clearly consistent and clearly understood, exist no longer. Unfortunately, some new ones that might serve to replace them have not as yet appeared. With what result? The meaning and purpose of contemporary religious life is fuzzy to many, and downright confusing to some.

Loss of identity

A number of factors gave rise to the rapid loss of identity experienced by the majority of U.S. religious since Vatican II. As mentioned earlier, decisions taken at that Council weakened the ideological foundation on which centuries of consecrated life had been built.[1] Our lack of role clarity—not having a clear sense of purpose and function within our Church—also intensified our problems with identity. *Vita Consecrata* states clearly that we are valued by the People of God for who we are rather than for what we do. But in recent years a number of us have found it difficult to answer convincingly this question: "What can we do that any lay person cannot?"

In addition, at least one other factor has helped shape the identity crisis in which a number of us find ourselves today. As noted briefly in Chapter I, we set out on our journey of renewal during a period of unusual social and political unrest in the U.S. The 1960's and 70's in the States are often referred to as the age of deconstruction. Americans took advantage of their newfound freedom to set about dismantling familiar structures in the life of the country. The family, organized religion, long-standing systems of governance were all systematically taken apart. Eventually, this process of deconstruction in the U.S. and the turmoil of the Church's post-Vatican II world converged. With what results? Among others, an unraveling of the existing forms and structures of religious life in the United States.

During the almost four decades in which old forms of consecrated life fell apart, other sweeping cultural shifts took place in the country. First of all, authority was democratized in America. In keeping with that development, a number of us, for the first time in memory, were given a significant role in the process of congregational decision-making.[2] Most of us were grateful for this innovation.

Within a short time, however, events began to move in directions that had not been anticipated. Some of us began to question the nature of authority and grew reluctant to give the last word to those who had been given responsibility to lead. Others of us, citing past abuses in this area, refused to endorse authority in any significant way.[3]

Second, in the years following Vatican II, many of us gave high priority to the challenge of personal growth. In so doing, we became better acquainted with principles of human development and psychology. For most of us this knowledge was of great help, but for a few, it led eventually to an excessive self-preoccupation, and a diminution of the impulse to generosity that typically marked our way of life.

Third, a number of our groups introduced the concept of a "personal call" to ministry. Over time, this innovation managed to erode, among some of our membership, any strong willingness to work on behalf of congregational goals. Those in this latter group raised questions about an understanding of vocation that entailed either obedience or discernment of God's will in the context of a congregational commitment.[4]

However, with this last point made, we must also admit that among some women's congregations, financial necessity, more than mission statements, determined ministry choice for many of their sisters. As mentioned earlier, years of selfless service with minimal remuneration left these groups with limited funds and few other assets available to pay for the care of their elderly and retired members. With fewer younger sisters in the group and an ever-growing number of older ones, some sisters simply had to find a job with an income that could support more than one community member.

Finally, as change occurred among U.S. religious, some of us began to be absorbed rapidly into the mainstream culture.[5] With what consequences? The sacrifice required to belong to a religious congregation decreased in relationship to the decline in vigor that once marked our way of life. We quickly found ourselves facing this challenge: how to reverse the process of assimilation, and thus remain distinctive in our world and Church. Eventually, we concluded that clearly re-defining membership's expectations would be part of that revitalization.[6]

A cause for concern

The current confusion about the place and purpose of religious in our Church and society is a worry for many people, lay and religious alike.[7] Timothy Radcliffe, OP, likens us to blacksmiths in a world of cars, wandering about looking for a new role.[8] The fact that the youngest members of our congregations appear to have the least understanding about what makes our way of life distinct is cause for particular concern.[9] Why? Because failure to gain some clarity about one's role leads more often than not to a growing sense of futility, reduced self-esteem, and a greater propensity to withdraw from consecrated life.[10]

Two examples illustrate the challenge we face. First, from January to June 1998, representatives of the National Religious Vocation Conference held more than 200 "listening sessions" with Catholic parents throughout the U.S. Their goal? To get an idea as to what mothers and fathers thought about contemporary religious life, and, their reaction should their son or daughter express an interest in joining a congregation. Participating parents reflected the theology and spirit of Vatican II, were committed to their faith, and active in their parish community. All of them had children who were young adults or younger.[11]

The results? These mothers and fathers reported a lack of information about consecrated life, and, like most people, were victims of the stereotypes of women and men religious that exist in the States today.[12] The authors of the report put it this way: Parents "are quick to admit they have no idea what priests, sisters and brothers do these days. They say most of their role models have disappeared."

Lack of knowledge on the part of parents, however, was not simply a lack of facts. Where, they asked, is the powerful and convincing emotional message about religious life that only personal testimony and witness provide? Where is the message that elicits admiration and a tears-in-the-eyes nod of understanding? Some parents went so far as to compare us to the anonymous members of a Twelve-Step Program: invisible as we go about doing good. "Not a single comment," wrote the report's authors, "shows any familiarity with what religious brothers are about these days. As for sisters, many parents have trouble identifying any 'value-added' quality to vowed religious life for women—they don't know what sisters do that their lay daughters can't do."[13]

Here is a second example. Donna Markham, OP, investigated the public image of religious priests and sisters; brothers were not included in the study. Her published results sobered those who read them: the lay men and women who participated in the study did not see religious so positively as the men and women religious saw themselves.[14] For example, in a self-rating, sisters described themselves as being a dynamic, active, powerful, and effective group; however, single women judged them to be rather good, but not very dynamic, and not any more progressive or effective than any of the other groups studied.

The investigation's results also raised serious concern about the long-term survival of many congregations of women religious in the U.S. Markham reports that despite a number of well-documented mission statements, ambiguity exists among a number of lay men and women, and many sisters themselves, about the mission of women religious in the States today. More than a few sisters were also discouraged about life in community, worried about falling short of serving the poor and disadvantaged adequately, and apprehensive about consecrated life's future. These preoccupations are symptomatic of what can be described as a "corporate depression."

However, many of the religious sisters in Markham's study reacted to this state of affairs by denying the seriousness of their situation. Several recommendations about further study and action were made on the basis of the investigation's results. Markham suggested, for example, that women religious take steps to insure that their mission is evident in both their way of life and their ministry. To achieve this end, she recommended that the role and mission of religious be clarified for congregational members and non-members alike.

Despite these and other examples, agreement continues to be far from uniform in the States about the importance of role clarity for contemporary consecrated life. Women religious are divided on the question. Asked whether or not their way of life differs from that of lay people, many sisters report no distinction.[15]

Where accord about a difference does exist, the reasons given to explain it sometimes do not help clarify the role of religious life in our Church. When asked whether or not consecrated life is distinct from the life lived by lay men and women, a few older religious priests cite ordination, rather than religious consecration and the evangelical counsels, as the source of difference.

Role clarity and the crisis of identity among religious brothers[16]

Role clarity, as we have mentioned, exists when I am aware of my purpose and function within any organization. The lack of role clarity, evident among some U.S. religious, has had a particularly corrosive effect on the identity of brothers. A number are not sure anymore what it means to be a member of a religious order in our contemporary Church. Though their vocation has always bewildered many people, since Vatican II religious brothers have suffered a greater loss of meaning than their ordained confreres. On the other hand, for good or ill, amidst four decades of head-spinning change in consecrated life, more than a few religious priests have relied upon their sacramental ministry for some stability and a sense of identity.

How explain the lack of a clear identity for brothers in today's Church? To begin with, during the years subsequent to the Council, many Catholics ceased to make a distinction between one congregation and another. Most sisters, religious priests, and brothers modified or put aside unique and widely recognized religious habits and took up a more uniform "lay" dress. As a result, their fellow Catholics lost not only one external and evident symbol of the fact that religious were different from the rest of the faithful, but also of the differences that existed between groups.

So also, as some moved away from their group's traditional ministry toward others judged to be more in keeping with the times, another long-standing and distinctive indicator of the difference between congregations disappeared. Over time, then, U.S. sisters, religious priests, and brothers became not only significantly less visible, but also moved toward greater apparent homogeneity. The phrase *generic religious* was coined to describe the end result of all these changes. Faced with this outcome and challenged to re-vision theoretically and theologically a distinct role for themselves within the ecclesial community, brothers floundered.

Second, while they hold a great deal in common with sisters and religious priests, brothers face unique challenges in terms of their identity. These spring from their singular position as male vowed religious who exercise their ministry through non-sacramental service. However, that fact has been obscured by the judgment, on the part of many, that men religious, priests and brothers alike, are part of some monolithic ecclesial structure. In reality, contemporary brotherhoods are multifaceted and pluralistic; diversity and an egalitarian manner of relating to others characterize their memberships. Brothers take offence when summarily dismissed as being part of a hierarchical and patriarchal male system of thought and action. While as men they have benefited from sexism in our society and Church, yet inasmuch as they are not members of the hierarchy, brothers are as marginalized as women in term of decision-making in our Church.

Third, brothers—who typically have ministered in institutions other than parishes—have somehow been lost in current discussions about Church ministry. These conversations focus commonly on the parish, judged by many to be the center of contemporary Church life. Though brothers have the potential to contribute significantly to current ongoing discussions about ministry, in general they are failing to do so today.

Finally, brothers are a pragmatic lot, and, prior to Vatican II, this characteristic served them well. As long as the basics of religious life were clearly defined, brothers knew what was expected of them in terms of the vows, spirituality, ministry, and community life. This knowledge gave them the freedom to get on with life in the monastery or with the daily work of their apostolate.

However, this system of meaning collapsed suddenly during the 1960's. Subsequently, brothers continued about their work, but without a clear understanding as to what the vows, spirituality, or community life required of them. Bruce Lescher of the Jesuit Theology School at Berkeley points out that the failure of brothers to acknowledge their system of meaning's collapse has given rise to a great deal of unspoken grief. Suggesting that they know how to repair wiring and plumbing better than how to rebuild meaning, Lescher concludes that the release of that grief will, for many brothers, be as painful as it is healing.

Differing opinions about religious life's state of health

If neither the public nor a number of men or women religious are clear about their role, confusion is also evident in the many reasons offered to explain U.S. religious life's general state of health at the moment. In a thoughtful analysis, for example, Sandra Schneiders, IHM suggests that recent studies of consecrated life, from the viewpoints of political philosophy,[17] cultural anthropology,[18] and organizational psychology, have been of limited help. They fail to explain fully the reasons for the steady attenuation that this way of living has experienced in the States during the past 40 years.[19]

Schneiders points out that most women religious with whom she has had contact do not exhibit those characteristics commonly found among people involved with a declining institution.[20] Few are cynical or overly self-involved. However, more than a few of these same women do report a profound malaise, or darkness, as they go about their day-to-day lives. This painful reality, Schneiders believes, is akin to a *dark night of the soul* as described by John of the Cross. Consequently, she concludes that their suffering is more hopeful. This she takes as a sign that a significant number of them are passing from a known and comfortable but somewhat immature stage of spirituality to a radically new experience of God.[21]

But other observers of contemporary consecrated life in the U.S., reading the same signs, come to different conclusions. They predict that the organizational decline of the past four decades will continue steadily unless we clarify our role and purpose as men and women religious in our Church and society, and make other significant changes in our way of living.[22] This second group cites the ever-increasing median age of religious, lack of new members, and diminished respect for contemporary religious life as evidence of its decline.[23]

How can we make sense of these two different points of view about religious life and its future in the U.S.? Might we not have here, as suggested in this book's introduction, a *both/and* rather than an *either/or* situation? Undoubtedly, a number of women religious, and some of their male counterparts, are passing through a dark night of the soul leading them to a radically new experience of God. At the same time, however, we must face a number of troubling facts that suggest that religious life, as an institution, grows ever more invisible and apparently inconsequential in contemporary U.S. society.

Denial in the face of diminishment

As mentioned above, Sandra Schneiders suggests that a need for conversion is a large part of the reason for the suffering and preoccupation evident among the members of many religious congregations in the U.S. today.[24] But a complementary explanation for their unrest is this troubling reality: from a purely secular point of view no organization can continue to carry out its mission without attracting new members and retaining those it already has.

If the statistics are to be believed, religious life in the U.S. is failing on both counts today. Many of us can readily accept Schneiders' line of reasoning. But are we equally willing to give ear to other more disagreeable and less hopeful explanations about the crisis in which U.S. consecrated life finds itself today?

The following example supports this last observation. Three years ago I received a phone call from a member of the General Council of a congregation of religious sisters. The caller asked if she and other Council members could meet with me to discuss the transfer of a young sister from one province to another. Apparently, the process got off to a good start, but was derailed when the receiving province began to raise questions about the sister seeking to move. I agreed to meet with five members of the Council.

During our meeting, members of the group often referred to the "young" sister who had requested the move. Eventually, I asked her age. Fifty-eight, I was told. My first thought? If this woman is a young sister, at what age does mid-life get underway in this congregation! At best, the woman in question is well past her mid-life transition. Some would go so far as to say that she is beginning to move into late adulthood. But of one thing we can be sure: she is certainly not a young person.

In congregations where there are few, if any, young members, those who joined the group with the unusually large novitiate classes of the 1960's, and are now in their late 50's and early to late 60's, have become perennial young religious. Though he or she might be flattered by the classification, identifying a 58-year-old man or woman as a young religious is one example of what Donna Markham means when she uses the term "denial."

The lack of role clarity among women and men religious today and their inability to face some troubling realities about their mission and life together have serious implications for consecrated life's identity and future.[25] Many lay men and women share the concerns that a number of sisters, religious priests, and brothers have about their place and purpose in our Church and world today. Together they ask, "Just what is the identity of contemporary religious life?"

Forming an identity

Forming an identity is never easy. On a personal level, we are all called to establish a provisional one during our adolescent and young adult years. We refashion that identity whenever we go through times of life change and transition. Surely, I am a different person at age 52 from the insecure young man who stepped onto the world's stage at 22. At that age, don't most of us feel as though we are impersonating an adult? Thirty years later, we feel all too adult indeed.

Men and women also approach the task of identity formation from different perspectives. Establishing boundaries in relationships often helps men with their self-definition. For women, relationships are more fluid and more central to the process of identity formation. Friendships with other women provide them with opportunities to share their inner world of meaning.[26] These different approaches to identity formation influence the ways in which men and women address the same task in the life of their congregations. Each gender has something to learn from the other.

What does it take for a congregation to develop a clear identity? *First of all, its members must take an honest look at the options available to them as a group.* Most congregations in the U.S. have been struggling to address this task since Vatican II. In light of our charisms and in response to the calls of the Church and world, changing realities, and new needs, we have asked: "Which ways of being in our world will foster a radical dependence on God and further the mission of Jesus?"

The second step in the process of identity formation includes dealing with the inevitable crises that follow upon any process of exploration. Over the past four decades, we have learned two hard lessons: exploration leads to crises, and the more possibilities for living that we uncover, the greater our number of crises.

The third and final step in the process of identity formation involves commitment. To bring any period of experimentation, change, and transition to fruition, we must make some choices. After assessing many competing and possibly equally compelling possibilities, we must decide where we stand, what points of view we hold, and how we plan to live our lives.

If we want to forge a new identity for our way of life, we cannot escape the process of assessment and choice. Although the expressions of religious life may be many and varied, in each of its manifestations we need to find certain fundamental components. Other groups face the same challenge as they struggle to define themselves. Take "family," for example. Though a range of groups—functional and dysfunctional—can claim the title "family" as their own, there comes a point where too few of the key elements that make up a family exist within a group for it to claim to be one.

In recent years, some men and women religious in the United States have failed to make the choices necessary to ensure that their identity and that of their congregation is clear to them and to everyone else.[27] If this situation continues, the meaning of religious life will be ambiguous. For example, some groups have broadened their understanding of congregational ministry to the extent that any work chosen by a member qualifies. Others are moving toward definitions of membership that will be so broad and all-inclusive that they have better application as descriptions of the Church at large than of a religious congregation. Observing these developments, young people considering their career and life choices are likely to judge a lifetime commitment to religious life as foolhardy.

False starts

Attempting to clarify consecrated life's identity, some women and men religious advocate re-establishing many past practices. They long for a return to the day when the tenets of this way of living were clear to anyone who took the time to think about it. They argue that the majority of contemporary U.S. religious have gone well beyond what the Fathers of Vatican II had in mind when they first encouraged renewal, and have essentially trans-formed their congregations into secular institutes.[28] Religious life in the United States is dying, this group contends. And is there any wonder why, they ask?

Undoubtedly, some elements of the past were set aside too quickly and must be reclaimed, in a way that respects the knowl-edge and experience gained during four decades of hard work adapting and renewing religious life. However, to retreat to mod-els that promoted vibrancy in another time, without also taking into consideration all that has been learned, would deny the overwhelming grace of renewal. Such a response to change is one way of achieving some closure during a time of uncertainty. But will choosing it, in the long run, further the work of forming a distinct and dynamic identity among religious in today's Church, or will it eventually lead to a loss of vitality and ultimately betray any possible future?

In the hard work of identity formation today, congregations need, at the outset, to ensure that Jesus is at the center of the life of the group and its members. They need also to reclaim the essentials of their foundress or founder's dream, and draw on the renewal experience of both individuals and the group over the past four decades. Since they are reworking their identity during a time when the prevailing image of religious life is also shifting, groups interested in a future for their life and ministry must also listen especially to the calls of the Church and the signs of the times in which we live.[29]

Today, as men and women religious, we face a twofold and formidable challenge: first, we need to respond creatively to the call to live out our passion for Jesus and the reign of God in the midst of diverse theologies and expressions of consecrated life. Second, we have an equally strong need to identify those elements that we, as God's people, believe must be commonly held by the groups who stake claim to this way of living.

The current crisis in religious life will not be resolved until everyone in our Church recognizes once again the characteristic identity of this way of living, as distinct from and equal to the diocesan priest and the lay person. To settle on just what makes up a distinct and fresh identity for consecrated life in the U.S. does not cut off the possibility of change in the future. It does, however, ensure that contemporary men and women religious stand for something.

Looking back over our recent history of risk-taking and hard work, and wanting to ensure the future vitality of our way of life, the time has come to ask this question: "In our efforts of the past 40 years, what has been of the Spirit and what has not?"

Reflection Questions

Following the format established at the end of earlier chapters, please spend some time reflecting on the following questions:

1. As you step away from Chapter III, with what feelings are you left? Does the viewpoint that you have just read make any sense to you as you reflect upon your own history and that of your congregation or province over the last 30 to 40

years? If yes, for what reasons does this point of view make sense? If no, for what reasons does it fail to hit the mark?

2. In light of the importance that a clear identity has for the future life and effectiveness of any group, are there major decisions related to the group's identity made by your congregation over the last 30 to 40 years that you want to reaffirm enthusiastically? Are there others that, in retrospect, you might question?

3. How would you respond should a young Catholic adult ask you this question: "Just who are (the name of your religious congregation), and for what do you stand?"

Notes

1 Fleming, "Understanding a Theology of Religious Life," 32.
2 Nygren and Ukeritis, *The Future of Religious Orders in the United States,* 246-247.
3 Ibid.
4 Ibid.
5 Ibid., 250.
6 Ibid.
7 Ibid., 248-249.
8 Timothy Radcliffe, OP, "The Bear and the Nun: the Sense of Religious Life Today," *Religious Life Review* 38:197 (July/August 1999), 194.
9 Nygren and Ukeritis, *The Future of Religious Orders in the United States,* 248-249.
10 Ibid.
11 Teresa Malcolm, "Study says parents won't push vocations," *National Catholic Reporter Online/archives* (September 11, 1998), http://www.natcath.com.
12 Kevin Axe, "Parent feedback: What it means for vocation ministers," *Horizon* 24:2 (Winter 1999), 3-6.
13 Malcolm, "Study says parents won't push vocations."
14 Donna J. Markham, "The Decline of Vocations in the United States: Reflections from a Psychological Perspective," in Laurie Felknor ed., *The Crisis in Religious Vocations: An Inside View* (Mahwah, NJ: Paulist Press, 1989), 181-196.
15 Nygren and Ukeritis, *The Future of Religious Orders in the United States,* 249.
16 This section draws heavily on an article by Bruce H. Lescher, CSC, "A Prologue to Brotherhood," in Michael F. Meister, ed., *Blessed Ambiguity: Brothers in the Church* (Winona, MN: St. Mary's Press, 1993), 7-26.

[17] Mary Jo Leddy, *Reweaving Religious Life: Beyond the Liberal Model* (Mystic, CT: Twenty-Third Publications, 1990).

[18] Gerald Arbuckle, *Out of Chaos: Refounding Religious Congregations* (Mahwah, NJ: Paulist Press, 1988).

[19] Sandra M. Schneiders, IHM, *Finding the Treasure: Locating Catholic Religious Life in a New Ecclesial and Cultural Context* (Mahwah, NJ: Paulist Press, 2000).

[20] Sandra M. Schneiders, "Contemporary Religious Life: Death or Transformation" in Cassian J. Yahaus, CP, ed., *The Challenge for Tomorrow: Religious Life* (Mahwah, NJ: Paulist Press, 1994), 9-34.

[21] Ibid.

[22] Nygren and Ukeritis, *The Future of Religious Orders in the United States,* 249.

[23] Timothy Radcliffe, OP, *Sing a New Song: The Christian Vocation* (Dublin, Ireland: Dominican Publications, 1999), 191-229; see also Nygren and Ukeritis, *The Future of Religious Orders in the United States.*

[24] Schneiders, "Contemporary Religious Life: Death or Transformation," 12-13.

[25] Nygren and Ukeritis, *The Future of Religious Orders in the United States,* 42-43.

[26] Seán D. Sammon, FMS, *An Undivided Heart: Making Sense of Celibate Chastity* (Staten Island, NY: Alba House, 1993).

[27] Patricia Wittberg, SC, *Creating a Future for Religious Life,* (Mahwah, NJ: Paulist Press, 1991); Patricia Wittberg, *The Rise and Fall of Catholic Religious Orders.*

[28] Ann Carey, *Sisters in Crisis: The Tragic Unraveling of Women's Religious Communities* (Huntington, IN: Our Sunday Visitor, 1997).

[29] Cada et al., *Shaping the Coming Age of Religious Life,* 59-60.

PERSONA
AND
PURPOSE

When pursuing a religious vocation, what does a young man or woman talk about? More often than not, a desire *to be more* like Christ, *to be closer* to Christ, and *to be of greater service* to Christ and his Church.[1] Not content with the quite heroic Christian life that most people choose to lead, he or she freely chooses to imitate Jesus' radical way of loving. Wouldn't we judge as foolhardy any young person who joined a religious congregation with the intention of doing as little as possible? The very identity of consecrated life includes a willingness to sacrifice.[2] For what purpose? To remind all of us about the requirements for a life of faith.

Religious life should exact a price from its members. Jesuit David Fleming suggests that an extraordinary generosity is necessary to respond to the call to this way of living.[3] The remarks of a young Australian Catholic affirm Fleming's line of reasoning. "When young people my age look into religious life," this young man stated, "they're searching for something that looks nothing like the world in which they live. We want to be challenged and transformed. Young people want something worth giving their lives for. If you want to attract young people to your Order, convince us that you can help us to live lives of greatness for Christ."[4]

Benedictine Sister Joan Chittister makes the same point when talking about Mother Sylvester, her first prioress.[5] The latter made two trips annually to the monastery's novitiate to pose but one question to those in formation: "Sisters, why have you come to religious life?" The novices' answers were predictable. "To give our lives to the Church," responded the pious. "To save our souls," ventured the cautious. "To change the world," insisted the zealous. With several sad shakes of her head, Mother Sylvester dismissed each and every response before providing her own: "Sisters," she said, "you come to religious life *only to seek God.*" Whatever new or renewed identity the People of God decide upon for consecrated life in the days ahead, at its heart must be this simple truth: religious life is all about finding God. For what other reason would it be worth the gift of your life?

Religious life defined

Since Vatican II, many of us have worked hard to assure fellow Church members that our way of life is no better than any other approach to living out the Gospel. And rightly so. However, in letting people know that we are just like everyone else, many of us have failed to address another equally important issue: what is it about our life that makes it unique?

Most theological and spiritual writers, in the years prior to the Council, answered that question by pointing to the vows of poverty, obedience, and chastity. The evangelical counsels, they said, are the sum and purpose of religious life.[6] But since Vatican II, our Church has emphasized the notion of *consecration* over the vows. Consecrated life is described as a call to imitate Jesus and his values more closely. Jesuit Marcello Azevedo puts it this way: the distinct character of religious life is the public profession by its members to live fully and radically the Gospel plan as the object of their life.[7]

Those of us who agree with this definition favor placing the word *consecration* at the heart of any renewed understanding of our way of life. Those among us who associate the term with the idea of setting someone or something apart for a sacred purpose, take exception to its use. But those in favor of using the word *consecration* argue that, by giving prominence to God's action, the term helps all of us avoid the temptation to see religious life as the creation and achievement of human beings. Instead, religious profession comes to be seen as the person's loving response to God's initiative.

Three elements

History teaches an important lesson. At the endpoint of any period of change and transformation in consecrated life, three familiar elements always seem to reappear, albeit in new forms: ministry, community, and spirituality. This outcome is no less true today. While the shape that they will take during the years to come can be discussed and debated, each of these elements appears foundational to any way of living that calls itself religious life.

The turmoil of the past 40 years has had a beneficial effect on the shape and structure of ministry, community, and spirituality, giving each of them the freedom to shed useless and burdensome historical trappings. The hard work of re-imagining these elements is a task that any congregation interested in a future cannot avoid. Each group lives them out in different ways. The word *community*, for example, gives rise to one image for a Jesuit priest and quite another for a Franciscan friar. Ministry is carried out in one way by the Sisters of Mercy of the Americas, and in quite another way by the members of a Carmelite community.

A final point before we move on. Those of us who live religious life know full well that the adventure of this way of living the Gospel is well worth the gift of anyone's life. As we move through the next few chapters, we will be looking at ways in which we can effectively get that "good news" out to the widest possible audience. The remainder of this chapter, however, is devoted to exploring the first of those three elements found at the heart of any renewed form of consecrated life: ministry. The other two will be addressed in Chapters V and VI respectively.

Mission and ministry

The mission of any congregation is an essential component of its identity. Mission has a twofold focus: the *Reign of God* as proclaimed by Jesus, and the *Church* that, ideally, is the sacrament and servant of that reign. Whenever our lives and actions promote the reign of God, we are on mission. Mission is not merely an activity of our Church; it constitutes its very being.

The chief characteristic of the Church's mission is prophecy. Prophets are people called by God and sent to remind us about this same God's saving interventions in the past. Prophets also challenge us to conversion in the present, and urge us to build up a new human community as God promised.[8] The sacrament of baptism is our call to mission, our invitation to be a prophet in the sense described above. As a consequence of our baptism, all of us who make up the People of God participate in Jesus' mission. Each and every Christian life involves a mission.

However, as women and men religious, we pledge ourselves to live out our baptismal commitment in a radical way. Consequently, our participation in the mission of Jesus must be revolutionary. Joan Chittister suggests as much when she points out that religious life must be lived in a way that reminds our world of what it can be, of what it must be, of what it most wants to be.[9]

Mission, ministry, and charism

The mission of Jesus gets lived out through specific ministries, and Saint Paul assures us that there are many of them. A group's charism serves an important function here in helping its members to determine their congregation's ministry. Yes, charisms do challenge and limit us. At the same time, they help us understand the difference in ministry between one group and another.

Apostolic religious congregations came into existence, in part, to meet one, or a range of, urgent and unmet human needs in the name of Jesus. The charism of any of our groups is an essential ingredient in the mix that is needed to determine its corporate ministry today, in light of the signs of the times and the calls of our Church. As we read those signs and listen to those calls carefully, our congregation's charism helps us answer this question: what works can honestly be judged to fall within our ministry?

Mission, ministry, and the poor

Consecrated life did not come into existence to eradicate poverty. If that were the sole rationale for this way of living the Gospel, then it should pass into history when and if the plight of the poor is alleviated. Clearly, however, congregations came into existence and will continue to flourish for many reasons in addition to the service their members may render to people who are poor.

In recent years, a great deal has been written and spoken—

often in moving and powerful ways—about the ministry of contemporary religious congregations and the poor who make up so much of our world's population. What is the relationship between the two? And, more important, where are we being called to put our efforts today as a group, in light of our charisms, vow of poverty, and the calls of our Church to serve the poor and others living at the margins of society?

In attempting to answer this question, we need, first of all, to be careful not to equate the practice of the vow of poverty with the plight of poor men and women.[10] There is an enormous difference, for example, between making a decision not to eat today, for one reason or another, and actually having nothing to eat. In light of my vow of poverty and a desire to identify with the poor of this world, for example, I might choose to eat but one meal each day for an extended period of time. In so doing, however, I must never forget this important fact: tomorrow there will be a meal for me—albeit but one. Can every poor person say the same thing with any assurance? Probably not. The most anyone of them might say is, "I wish I could have eaten something today, and only God knows whether I will get anything to eat tomorrow." These are two radically different experiences. We patronize the poor when we persuade ourselves that, because of our vow of poverty, we share their plight. We have a freedom that women and men who are poor do not.[11]

In discussions about poverty, many of us also fall into a second trap: we speak about or relate to poor men and women as though they were a category of people rather than specific persons who happen to be impoverished. Groups of people classified as poor are made up of individual adults and/or children. Each and every one of them has his or her hopes and dreams, frustrations and disappointments, gifts and graces, and selfishness and sin—just like the rest of us. Relating to people who are poor as though they were a class of people, rather than individuals, creates an artificial distance between them and us, and transforms any experience of immersion in a situation of impoverishment into little more than "tourism among the poor."

Should the vast majority of men and women religious in the U.S. today give priority to ministry among the poor? Of course we should. The Church at large has encouraged our Orders in this direction for a number of years. At their 1971 Synod, the participating bishops called for action on behalf of justice as a *constitutive dimension of preaching the Gospel.* Work with the poor is part of the spirit of the founding charism of most of our apostolic congregations, and an extraordinary number of General and Province Chapters have taken decisions that would orient our groups more fully toward service to men, women, and young people in situations of impoverishment. What additional encouragement is necessary?

Today, if we have not already done so, we need to put aside the rhetoric that can so often dominate discussions about serving impoverished individuals. We need, instead, to imagine what a creative and courageous response to this challenge might look like, in the concrete situations in which our congregations find themselves. We would also benefit from examining the relationship that exists between the original ministry of our congregations and the ever-increasing population of the world's poor.

Patricia Wittberg, SC, adds one other observation worth our consideration: among young women and men religious today, ministry to the poor is where their hearts lie.[12] Contrary to the stereotype that the "Baby Boomer" generation is the most socially involved of all age groups, those who come after them express a wish to live with the poor, to serve the poor in their ministry, and to promote social justice as a core value for their congregations.

Identity's transforming power

Groups hoping for a future must attend to this important aspect of identity: fidelity to their founding person's impulse to address urgent and unmet human needs in the name of Jesus. Why? Because this facet of their identity, their ministry, has the potential to galvanize and, over time, transform any congregation. The following example illustrates this point.

By charism and tradition, the sisters of a century-old congregation in the eastern part of the U.S. had served the needs of women. Consequently, their group decided to rededicate one of its nearly abandoned inner-city facilities to educating women who had not completed their high school diploma requirements. As the sisters began to assess the program's needs, they discovered that many of the women, lacking child-care opportunities, often brought their children with them to the program. The children needed to be cared for while the women studied.

A child-care center was established. But in short order, that facility's staff discovered that a number of the children were malnourished, and a few were abused or drug addicted. Emergency treatment was obtained for these children by networking with one of the congregation's hospitals located in a neighboring suburb. Eventually, a health clinic was established on the school site to provide medical services and nutritional counseling.

Within a year of the overall project's foundation, 12 sisters, all members of the congregation that had set it up, asked to be assigned to its staff. To make this move, most left individual ministries, similar in nature to the program they were joining. Their willingness to enter together into this corporate work enabled their congregation to carry out the ministry for which it was founded. By their community witness the sisters achieved together a level of effectiveness that had escaped them in their individual ministries.[13]

If we plan on a future for our congregation, we must be crystal clear about our group's identity and specific about its ministry. To arrive at this outcome, we will have to make some hard choices. Those of us willing to do so, however, will come to understand just what we stand for and what makes us different from other groups in our Church. Eventually, everyone outside our group will also grasp these two important distinctions.

Corporate commitments

A religious congregation establishes its corporate identity when its members decide upon a focus for the life of the group.[14] This decision does not imply that everyone must be engaged in the same ministry or live and work in the same place. It does, however, insure that anyone who looks at the group can quickly answer the question, "What is this congregation known for?"

Subsequent to the Council, the leaders of a number of congregations expanded previously held understandings about their group's ministry. This development was in keeping with the spirit of the times and the challenge to find new ways to meet new needs and to address new realities. As a consequence, some of us were permitted to take up works that—while still falling within the definition of our group's primary ministry—were different from the traditional involvements of our congregation. In other groups, for a variety of reasons, some few members also took up ministries other than the one for which their group was founded.[15]

Due in part to these developments, a sense of *being sent* by our congregations began to erode over time among many of us. The leadership of some of our groups also found themselves less capable of making corporate commitments to ministries that addressed compelling and unmet human needs, needs quite similar to those that had so captured our founding persons' hearts and moved them to action. Our leaders simply lacked available personnel.

A scenario such as the one described above can become self-defeating for any of our congregations. Why? *Because the vitality and viability of our groups depend upon their ability to demonstrate a consistent reason for existing and to engage in a credible corporate mission.*[16] Apostolic congregations came into being, in large measure, to meet concrete needs. Whether it was to care for the indigent, educate and evangelize the sons and daughters of immigrants, or shelter the homeless, some ministry lay at the heart of their founding moment.

One of the great strengths of these orders has been the members' ability to address any of these needs as a group. For a congregation to develop a statement of mission or charism broad enough to include any work chosen by a member undermines that group's potential for developing a ministry vision that is commonly held and deeply shared by the membership. Over time, the congregation and its leadership will find corporate commitments becoming nearly impossible to maintain.[17] With what result? The ministry for which God called the congregation into existence might very well go undone.

From time to time, of course, one or another of our congregations will free up and send forth a member for a work of the Church that falls outside the group's overall ministry. Someone, for example, has specialized training for which a diocese or the Church, on a regional or national level, has an urgent and immediate need. With the blessings of the congregation's leadership, this person sets about this work of the Church, and, for a period of time, is not engaged in the congregation's ministry.

Painful and challenging as we might find the exercise, we need to ask ourselves two questions today. Are we committed to the dream of our foundress or founder? Do we plan to channel a significant portion of our energies toward realizing it—even though in response to new needs in a changed reality? If the majority of us in any one group answer "no" to either inquiry, we will have little reason to wonder whether or not our congregation and its mission have a future. In all probability, neither will last much beyond our group's present generation of members.

Fresh and creative approaches to ministry

In addressing the important area of ministry, we need not retreat to models more suitable for the past. Nor should we respond solely to the ministry needs of the local church, as pressing as those might seem. Instead, we can live out the founding vision of our congregation in fresh and creative ways. To do so, however, some questions must be asked. First, what are the essential components of our group's founding ministry—to evangelize the young, especially the poor; to provide health care in a spirit of mercy; to spread the Gospel message using communications media? Each of our congregations must work to reach consensus on the elements that define its ministry.

Next, to what urgent human need was our group responding at the time of its foundation, and how is that need present in our world today? As religious, we have typically gone to places where we could work with people whom society had cast aside. Adequate educational and health care facilities exist in many parts of the United States today because men and women religious first provided them when the larger society would not.

We also need to ask what target group was identified for our services at the very beginning. Was it children and women at risk? The elderly? Those in need of catechizing? The homeless? Those denied adequate medical care? A yet unserved population? Of course in all of this, our congregations have to determine realistically what human and financial resources they must have on hand in order to meet this need in its new form.

The following example illustrates the points just made. A group of women religious in the southeastern region of the United States administered an elementary school. Among their pupils were a large number of children of migrant workers. Many of these students spent but a few weeks at the school before moving on with their families to follow the harvest.

Three of the religious who served at the school decided to follow up on these children to determine the consequences of the frequent moves to which they were subjected. They discovered that a significant percentage of the students dropped out of school entirely after three or four moves. This was not surprising: what elementary-school child can sustain several "new beginnings" each academic year?

The solution these women religious devised for this problem shows that a congregation's foundational ministry can adapt to new needs. With the blessing of their province leadership team, they bought three mobile homes, used them to set up a school and a community, and moved with the migrant children. With what results? Among others, a significantly lower dropout rate at the end of one year.

Similar examples abound of creative and fresh applications of a congregation's foundational ministerial vision to contemporary needs. Consider the Alexian Brothers, a congregation of men religious who trace their origins back to the Middle Ages.[18]

This group's members first came into prominence because of their care for victims of the Black Death that struck Europe in 1346. At great risk to their lives, these men nursed people suffering from the epidemic and abandoned by family. They also buried those who succumbed to the disease. Today, as part of Alexian Brothers Health System in the U.S., the congregation has set up centers such as Bonaventure House, an assisted-living residence in Chicago, Illinois for persons with AIDS. And so, they continue to serve women and men often marginalized by the rest of society.

The recent joint effort of several congregations of men and women religious to establish a school in inner city Baltimore to serve at-risk minority students is yet another example of innovations in ministry on the part of several groups working cooperatively. Pooling their resources and initiating a development effort at the outset, they staffed the school with a significant number of sisters and brothers. They also took steps to minimize costs, thus putting the price of Catholic education within reach of the economically poor. More important, the children attending the school now have access to services that the state and other organizations had failed to provide.

Citing as examples Catholic schools and other Church institutions, does not rule out the possibility of new and innovative ministries emerging among some groups. We have seen this phenomenon occur before. During the years subsequent to the French Revolution, appreciable numbers of women in active religious orders for the first time in history left their cloisters and engaged in apostolates. Which ones? The only two in which women were tolerated at the time: teaching and nursing. Consequently, for sisters in our time any revitalization of religious life will obviously include a range of apostolates in addition to teaching and nursing. These new undertakings will be found to be just as important, even if they are novel for us now, as nursing and teaching were a century and a half ago.[19]

A final point. Amata Miller, IHM, in a video presentation of the project *Threads for the Loom: LCWR Planning and Ministry Studies,* suggests that, as religious, one of the unique contributions we can make today in ministry is in our commitment to a geographic area.[20] How many other people are able to guarantee the 20 or more years that might be needed to insure significant transformation in a neighborhood, outreach programs for juvenile offenders, and so forth? While personnel might change at times, a congregation's long-term commitment assures those being served that the larger group will see the program through to completion.

The role of institutions

In recent years, some of us have come to regard institutions with suspicion. With good reason. To remain vital, every institution must from time to time undergo a process of transformation. Most also need to be reminded periodically about the reason for their foundation. Unfortunately, none of us can guarantee that any institution will avail itself of these necessary corrective measures.

Institutions, though, have the potential to be powerful means of social change. They also give those of us who are religious two other advantages. One, we have greater visibility in the community. Two, most institutions provide us with a place where we can come into contact with young people who might have an interest in joining our congregations.

During the process of renewal that has been underway since Vatican II, a number of us determined that our group's service in one or another institution had run its course. We passed on to others the responsibility for these foundations. In retrospect, however, some of our groups may have moved on too quickly from some institutional commitments. In so doing, we not only lost a point of contact with the young, but also our ability to set the future direction of these facilities in keeping with our congregation's charism.

Let's keep this fact in mind: institutions that continue faithful to their founding vision and those that can be transformed so as to be more responsive to the signs of the times can be a valuable resource to the members of any religious congregation.

The witness of serving together

Several times now we have pointed out that radical Gospel living in a religious congregation exacts a price. Ideally, those of us who choose freely to live the Gospel radically become deeply involved in the life of our congregation. In so doing, we allow our sisters and brothers in religious life, and the group as a whole, a significant claim over our person, time, and talents.

We must admit, however, that for a number of our congregations in the U.S. today, a gap exists between the group's stated ideals and our ability to realize them. Valuable aspects of identity were lost when a few among our membership migrated to the periphery of our congregations and took up a variety of important but individual ministries. Despite their contributions in ministry, some of these sisters, brothers, and religious priests have ended up having little involvement with their congregations or with consecrated life itself.[21]

Religious congregations are social groups.[22] Consequently, we have greater potential for effectively carrying out the ministry of our groups when we work together. In hospitals, schools, shelters, legal centers, and so forth, people united in a common effort and working side by side have an impact more significant than that achieved by most individual initiatives. Corporate commitments, even when they are short-term, appear to make a statement about a group and its nature that individual involvements do not.

New models of religious life may well be emerging in the United States where elements other than a common mission, life together, and spirituality bind a group of people and help them make sense of their commitment to the Gospel. However, our congregations must continue to give priority to—and support actively by word and deed—those among our members who wish to pursue together a common and corporate ministry as they work to breathe new life into our original founding inspiration.

Selfless service

As apostolic religious, we are called to a life of service. What comes to mind when you or I think of the word *service*? Several images: sharing our time, talents, and education with others; or having a spirit of generosity; or providing care for children, the aged and infirm, or some other group. And, in fact, all these examples fall under the heading of service.

Accepting the fact that service has an altruistic side to it is easy. Not so easy, however, is acknowledging this reality: someone who performs a service may be doing so out of self-interest. People in political life, for example, are not known for performing their service selflessly. At the very least, most of them hope that any favor that they do for a constituent will result in one more vote on election day. We have come to expect this type of behavior from politicians and, indeed, such ambitions are not wrong for people in the political world.[23]

While we are usually educated for one profession or another, as religious we are, first and foremost, apostles. Certainly, we should have the necessary credentials in our field of work. But Jesus and his message, and a spirit of selfless service must be our motivation, much more than a need for success. In taking on an attitude of selflessness or disinterest, we insure that it is the Gospel of Jesus and not ambition that enlivens us in our ministry. When it comes to the spiritual life, those with a spirit of *disinter-*

est are not uninterested. Instead, they place the focus on others rather than on themselves.

As religious, we are invited to enter into the Paschal Mystery, and to live out in our everyday life the dying and rising of Jesus. As with any call to love, the call to religious life is an invitation to surrender, to imitate Christ in his pattern of self-emptying, so as to be transformed fully by divine life.

For Jesus, there was no self-seeking or ambition in his preaching, in his miracles and healing, nor in his arguments with the Pharisees and Sadducees. As religious, we are called to follow his example. We have a responsibility to witness more fully and more intensely to who Jesus is. Failing to remain true to our choice of radically identifying with Christ, we become but another group of political or social activists. As religious, we must stand out in both Church and world for the selfless service we render in Christ's name.[24]

The problem of assimilation into parish life

Our steady and widespread move, in recent years, into diocesan and parochial positions has, in some instances, also had a detrimental impact on the identity of our way of life. As mentioned earlier, apostolic religious life has typically risen up in the Church to serve urgent or unmet human needs. As a consequence, historically, our congregations have been independent of, but complementary to, the hierarchical structure of the Church.[25]

However, the decreased number of secular clergy today, at a time when the parish is defined as the primary locus of ecclesiology, has led to an increasing dependence on religious orders of priests to staff diocesan operations. Religious sisters and brothers in the States have also been pressed into service administering parishes and taking up other roles that have not traditionally been theirs. This development, as well as the decline in the number of institutions sponsored by our congregations, has compromised the prophetic role that religious life plays in our Church.[26] To remain faithful to our charism and purpose, we need to re-examine this development and redirect our efforts where necessary.

At the same time, we must admit that some older sisters and brothers have taken up parochial positions for various practical reasons. Forced to retire from teaching or health care ministry, some have taken a parish position so as to remain active. Thus, they continue to make a contribution to the Church as a whole, and to their institutes and those they serve as well.

Partnership with lay men and women

Ongoing collaboration between religious and lay women and men witnesses to the fact that our Church is capable of an ecclesiology of communion. Today this witness is more important than ever. All too often, past Church actions have betrayed a power-controlled ecclesiology—an outcome antithetical to Gospel principles.[27] As religious, we must, through our life and work together, bear witness to the fact that it should and can be otherwise.

Close collaboration in ministry between ourselves and lay men and women is an important part of our congregations' mission today. As mentioned earlier, charisms are gifts of the Spirit given to our Church, and not the personal property of the members of one religious order or another. Ministry is an area in which lay people and religious can share a great deal.

Are we willing to enter into partnership in ministry with our lay colleagues? Can we discuss together what is best for the institutions that we steward together, for those they serve, for the long-range goals of their ministry? More important, after that conversation, can we act in the best interest of all involved when appointing leaders or developing teams of people to address the pressing needs that make up the ministry of so many congregations? This area is a painful one for many religious and lay people alike. Unspoken issues of power and politics, on both sides, can derail discussion and subvert any genuine progress that might be made. The Gospel of Jesus must be our guide as we move ahead.

In partnership with lay people we can point the way toward the future face of the Church. Both groups have a unique opportunity to share spirituality and ministry with one another. In so doing, we give witness to what our Church can and must be. But as communities of religious, we will be able to rise to this challenge only if we have a strong sense of identity and a sufficient number of active members for genuine partnership.

Some final thoughts

What must we do to assure a vital and viable future for our congregations and their mission? We need, first of all, to place Jesus and his Gospel at the center of our life. It is the Lord, ultimately, who will move us to respond generously to urgent human needs in keeping with our founding purpose.

Second, by our choice of corporate ministries, our style of life, and our public witness, we need to stand against those values in U.S. culture that undermine radical personal and institutional conversion. Today, they include individualism, materialism, consumerism, and a lack of respect for human life.

Make no mistake about it: genuine renewal of consecrated living in the U.S. will, over time, move us to the margins of our society. The will of God, undoubtedly, is what will determine the outcome of our efforts to renew religious life in the States.

However, at the same time, we must begin to reverse the process underway to assimilate our way of life into U.S. culture, and strive instead to be recognized primarily by our obvious joy in serving God, simplicity of life, and visible presence among those most abandoned by society.

This task will be a challenging one. Since the beginning of our nation, American Catholics have worked to put to rest the recurring myth that being a good Catholic and a good citizen are somehow antithetical. However, today by our choice of ministry and style of life, we must call into question many of the values so evident in our nation and culture. Our public commitment to live more intensely the evangelical counsels is a first step in that direction. By vowing to hold all goods in common, live out our human sexuality in a celibate chaste manner, and allow our congregations considerable claim over our time, talents, and energies, we witness to values that differ from those held by many of our fellow citizens.

In carrying out our ministry in a spirit of selfless service, we witness further to counter-cultural values. How? By avoiding the all too familiar and tragic betrayal of consecrated life that occurs when we give our heart away generously at the time of first commitment, and then take it back, bit by bit, with each passing year.

Throughout religious life's recent 40-year period of change and turmoil, there have consistently been fellow religious in our midst who, regardless of their age, were aware of the distinctiveness of their vocation to religious life. In setting them alongside others of us whose willingness to sacrifice for the common good has diminished in recent years, one critical challenge of renewal quickly becomes apparent. The future of U.S. consecrated life hinges, in part, upon the ability of the members of our various congregations to choose between the high cost of Gospel living and the demands of an exclusively private understanding of vocation to religious life.[28]

Reflection Questions

1. For what reason did your religious congregation come into existence? What, for example, was the original dream of your founder or foundress and how is that dream being lived out today? What changes need to occur in the overall structure of your group, the daily life of its members, and in your life personally so that the foundress or founder's dream is vital and vibrant throughout the 21st century?

2. How willing are you personally to make these changes? How willing do you think your congregation or province might be to make them? How might you alert your congregation to your concerns and, by so doing, influence some small change? What consequences will you face personally for taking action one way or another?

Notes

[1] Fleming, "Understanding a Theology of Religious Life," 42.
[2] Ibid., 43.
[3] Ibid., 42-43.
[4] Quoted in the *Marist News* 8 March 2000, Province of New Zealand, 10.
[5] Joan Chittister, *The Fire in These Ashes* (Kansas City, MO: Sheed & Ward, 1995) 44-45.
[6] Fleming, "Understanding a Theology of Religious Life," 23.
[7] Marcello Azevedo, *Vocation for Mission: The challenge of religious life today* (Mahwah, NJ: Paulist Press, 1988).
[8] Michael Amaladoss, SJ, "The religious in mission," in Union of Superiors General, ed., *Consecrated Life Today: Charisms in the Church for the World* (Middlegreen, Slough: St. Pauls, 1994), 131.
[9] Joan Chittister, OSB, "Religious in the Evangelizing Mission of the Church" (Rome, USG, 1993), 28-29.
[10] Michael Himes, "Returning to our Ancestral Lands," *Review for Religious* 59:1 (January/February 2000), 20-24.
[11] Ibid.
[12] Patricia Wittberg, SC, "What to expect from Generation X," *Catholic Vocations: Melbourne Archdiocese* 3:1 (March 2000).

[13] Nygren and Ukeritis, *The Future of Religious Orders in the United States,* 238-239.

[14] Miriam Ukeritis, "Religious Life's Ongoing Renewal: Will Good Intentions Suffice?" *Review for Religious* 55:2 (March/April 1996), 118-132.

[15] Ibid., 127-128.

[16] Nygren and Ukeritis, *The Future of Religious Orders in the United States,* 244-251.

[17] Leddy, *Reweaving Religious Life,* 73.

[18] Felix Bettendorf, CFA, "Contemporizing a Charism: The Alexians Opt for AIDS Ministry," *CMSM Forum* 56 (Spring-Summer 1990), 1-9.

[19] Ibid., 14-15.

[20] Cited in Ukeritis, "Religious Life's Ongoing Renewal: Will Good Intentions Suffice?", 129.

[21] Nygren and Ukeritis, *The Future of Religious Orders in the United States,* 244-246.

[22] Wittberg, *Creating a Future for Religious Life,* 1.

[23] Fleming, "Understanding a Theology of Religious Life," 46-48.

[24] Ibid.

[25] Nygren and Ukeritis, *The Future of Religious Orders in the United States,* 250-251.

[26] Ibid.

[27] Charles Howard, FMS, *Remarks delivered at the Marist Africa Conference,* Nairobi, Kenya (August 1992).

[28] Nygren and Ukeritis, *The Future of Religious Orders in the United States,* 246.

RE-IMAGINING COMMUNITY LIFE

One day a wise old rabbi asked his students, "How can you tell that night has ended and the day is returning?"

"When you can see clearly that an animal in the distance is a lion and not a leopard," suggested one. "No," answered the rabbi.

"Could it be," asked another, "when you can tell that a tree across the field bears figs and not peaches?" Once again, the rabbi replied, "No."

Growing impatient, his pupils demanded, "Well, then, what is it?"

"It is when you can look on the face of any person and see that that woman or man is your sister or brother. Because until you are able to do so, no matter what time of day it is, it is still night."

This disarming tale has some implications for understanding life in a religious community.

Contemporary community life

To begin with, every community is flawed in one way or another. That observation should come as no surprise. You and I are not perfect, and neither are those with whom we live. And neither is any human community. Different perceptions about the nature of community life, the day-to-day disagreements that occur in the lives of all of us, and, at times, the failure of those with whom I live to meet my expectations can lead to disappointments and hurt feelings. As a consequence, a spirit of reconciliation must be at the heart of the everyday life of any religious community that claims to have moved from darkness toward the light.

How best define community life in a religious congregation? One way, perhaps one of the best ways, certainly one of the most honest ways, is to simply say it is an affair of the heart. Life together with our brothers and sisters challenges you and me, first and foremost, to form and nurture a loving heart.[1] Without that, we will survive, but never flourish in community.

For too many of us, mere mention of the word *community* gives rise to an entirely different set of responses. We often find ourselves defensive, resistant, and silent. We know well, for example, some very rational reasons for living outside the communities of our province or congregation. Some of us maintain that community doesn't necessarily mean life together under the same roof, and point to our colleagues at work, or our family, or a circle of friends as our source of support.

When faced with questions about the nature and purpose of community life, some of us fall back on the law. Quoting those articles in our congregation's constitutions that bear upon the matter, we insist that there is but one way to live out community life. Read the rules, we say; they are quite clear and allow for few exceptions.

Still others among us, pointing to some obviously troubled religious community as an example, protest that we are no longer willing to tolerate what we judge to be a dysfunctional way for adults to live together. "I don't want to live any longer with people who are crazy," we say.

Some few of us seek to live alone. We cite the pressures of ministry or, having been hurt in the past by rigid structures and the inappropriate exercise of authority, we have concluded that living alone protects us from getting hurt once again and we claim, in the long run, is simply easier.

There are also those of us who feel overwhelmed by community life or lack the skills necessary to cope with a diverse and challenging group of adults living together physically. We choose instead to merely co-exist with those with whom we share the house. With what result? Loneliness, irritability, and ongoing disappointment.

Community life is often described in Church and congregational documents as a mainstay of consecrated life. But for many of us, it has become, instead, one of the thorniest issues that we have had to face since the Council.

With all this bad news, we must wonder: is there a value today in community living? Of course there is! However, if truth be told, most of us are ambivalent about facing life together. Yes, you and I want the support, the care, and the affirmation that can be found in the common life. At the same time, we are often reluctant to change familiar and long-standing behavior patterns or to allow our group some claim over our time, talents, and resources. Let's also admit that it is easy to point to many aspects of community life that are unattractive. How much more difficult, though, for us to acknowledge that being called together by God is what transforms our life in community into a moment of grace.

What religious communities are not

Community life is easy to define in the abstract. But giving structure and form to it in the concrete circumstances of our everyday life is considerably more challenging. Throughout the history of consecrated life, several models describing the nature and purpose of community have been used to help us with this task. While one or another of them may have been useful in their day, most appear to be of little help at the moment.

Some of us, for example, have been encouraged to think of our community as a family. Various images from Scripture and Tradition have been employed to support this viewpoint, with an idealized picture of life among the Holy Family at Nazareth heading the list. While life together in a community can bear witness to some positive aspects of family life, a religious community is definitely not a family.

A family, by its very nature, includes relationships between people of unequal status and power. Consider, for a moment, the exasperated mother of a rebellious 18-year-old who disciplines her son with these words: "As long as you continue to live under this roof, you will do as I say and follow the rules of this house!" Such a relationship is hardly marked by mutuality and equal levels of independence.

Use of a family model to describe religious community life has also given rise to hierarchical structures not in keeping with the nature of consecrated life. Haven't we in the past referred to at least one member of the community as "Mother" or "Father" Superior? Is it any wonder, then, that other members over time regressed to behavior patterns more suitable to an earlier age in life, or simply rebelled, projecting onto the community's leader all their unresolved issues with parents and other authorities.

Religious communities are also not therapeutic communities. There are, of course, healing aspects to our life together. We can unburden ourselves to one another, and, where the members of the group are mature and generous, mutual support is forthcoming. While a religious community can and must be a place where we thrive humanly and spiritually, the personal growth of its members can never be the primary reason for its existence.

In contrast, the chief concern of a therapeutic community is the personal growth of its members. The individual and his or her needs have a prominent place. Free of most external distractions, the members of these communities spend considerable time discussing life within the group and their own conduct. With what results? Helpful insights into the reasons for their behavior and a better understanding of the impact that it has on others.

Our religious communities were founded so we could live the Gospel and proclaim the Word of God. Our primary mission is to love God and to make God known and loved. The world outside the community, then, is our proper focus. Our life together supports us so that we can carry out our congregation's mission. In applying the model of a therapeutic community to religious life, we run the risk of turning our group's focus inward, thus promoting unrealistic expectations about the community and its members, and distorting the true nature and purpose of Gospel-based community living.

Religious communities as groups

With that said, we must also admit that since Vatican II, the discipline of psychology has helped many of us understand more fully some of the emotional and interpersonal aspects of our life in common. Knowledge about differences in personality, the help many of us received in identifying and expressing feelings, and skills training in communication have gone a long way toward improving the quality of life in a number of groups.

More recently, however, Patricia Wittberg, SC, has reminded us that sociology too has something to say about community life. Psychology, she points out, most often has the individual in mind. In contrast, sociology is focused on the group, a term that describes a situation where three or four unrelated persons come together and interact on a somewhat permanent basis. The principles of sociology, then, would lead us to conclude that while not every social group is a religious community, an important dimension of any religious community is the fact that it is a *social group*.[2] And just as our spiritual growth is conditioned by our psychological make-up, so too, the social dynamics of our congregation help determine its ability to live out our founding person's charism and respond creatively to our Church's challenge to adapt and renew itself.

Social groups are no simple matter. They come in all sizes and shapes, and serve a variety of purposes. At the office, or as a member of a school faculty or parish team, I belong to a work group.[3] The common task that has drawn my colleagues and me together gives definition to this type of community.

A group can be defined also by the degree of commitment it asks. In an *intentional community*, for example, I freely commit myself to live, work, pray, and relax with a specific group of people. Do I pay a price for membership in this type of community? Of course. The group makes extensive demands on my time and energy. I also learn quickly that its transcendent mission takes precedence over my needs and those of other community members.[4]

Common practices and traditions, and a spirit of sacrifice and mortification characterize intentional communities. They also have clear boundaries that reinforce the distinction between those who belong to the group and those who do not.

Prior to Vatican II, there appeared to be no other kind of religious community except an *intentional community*. Sacrifice bonded us to our particular congregation: we were required to dress in a certain way, take up particular works without consultation, accept the superior's will, and follow what might, in retrospect, be benignly described as a rigid daily schedule.

From the time of initial formation, rituals and routines— many dating back to the time of the founding person—also marked the life of our congregations. Certain feast days were celebrated, particular customs observed, and chapters of faults held. People outside the group were referred to as *externs,* and contact with those who had left the community was discouraged.

Since the Council, however, some of our religious communities have developed in such a way that they more closely resemble two other types of social groups: bureaucracies and associations. This situation is evident in both local communities and the world of the congregation at large.

In *bureaucracies,* we are assigned specific roles and tasks. Our contribution to the community is measured by our ability to fulfill these roles and carry out these tasks. Job descriptions, therefore, take on an importance that far exceeds their usefulness. A familiar phrase that you hear from time to time in any group classified as a bureaucracy is, "It's not my job!"

In adopting the language and structures of a bureaucracy, some congregations have taken on a corporate or commercial culture rather than that of a Gospel-based community. The "Provincial," for example, suddenly became the "President." Job interviews replaced the annual appointment list; assignment to a local community now required an application and an interview.

In retrospect, when we decided to restructure our models of governance and animation, rather than adopting classifications and categories found helpful in business and commerce, we might have done better to create a new vocabulary along with new models. Such a development would have been more in keeping with our experience of leadership and the common life over the past four decades. Religious life is not a 9 A.M. to 5 P.M. operation. Often, the roles that are most essential to each of our groups are also those we are least able to measure accurately.

An *association* is the second type of group that some congregations began to resemble during the years after the Council. Associations require the most limited commitment from their members. Belonging to the local bowling league, for example, will hardly make significant demands on my time and energy.

As a member of an association, I invest a certain amount of my resources in the group so as to attain some common goal or objective. At the same time, however, I retain my personal autonomy. This arrangement confuses many young people considering religious life as a vocation. For example, they ask: "Just when did living alone as a permanent arrangement, finding my own employment, and deciding independently on the use of almost all my free time, with only tangential contact with my religious congregation, stop being called the 'single life' and become just another form of community?" Religious congregations that move in the direction of establishing themselves as associations run the risk of not lasting beyond their current generation.

Stages in the growth of any community

Psychiatrist Irvin D. Yalom, MD, identifies four stages in the formation of any community.[5] First of all, those of us who will make up the group must come together or *form*. During this stage we are usually on our best behavior. Polite and solicitous about the needs of others, we keep to ourselves many of our negative opinions about the group and its members.

Not so during what Yalom calls the second, or *storm*, stage of community formation. Members of any group that is healthy

and has the possibility of further growth must be able to disagree, at times heatedly, and to resolve their differences in a
mutually acceptable manner. Unfortunately, false notions about
what the virtue of charity entails have rendered many of us inca-
pable of telling the truth. Instead, we remain silent to keep the
peace.

The virtue of charity, however, is practiced when I speak
the truth out of my respect for you. I do so whether that truth is
good news or bad news. I don't have to tell you all the truth, at
least as I see it, at one time, but charity requires that I speak the
truth.

Likewise, remaining silent and allowing a person who is
angry, withdrawn, or abusing alcohol to control the community
with his or her behavior has little to do with Gospel living. In
failing to take action, all of us who make up the group eventually become crippled. Remember: communities are systems. What
happens in the life of one person has ramifications for all of us in
the group. While we generally prefer to classify the person caus
ing all the trouble as the identified patient, in remaining silent
we all collude in and add to the group's dysfunction.

Learning to disagree and to resolve differences are skills
that can be acquired. And learn them we must! What other alternative do we have? To wring our hands in despair about the state
of our religious community? Such behavior, as we well know,
will do little to change the quality of life within the group.

During the third stage in the formation of any group, *norms*
are established. Having agreed that it is safe to disagree, community members can speak honestly about their hopes and disappointments and arrive at a consensus about the details of their
life together. Who will manage the group's finances? How often
and in what manner will we pray in common? What responsibilities do we have to one another? These are but a few of the
many questions we must address.

Obviously, the constitutions and statutes of our religious congregation have an important role to play at this stage. If we are looking for a community that will be a source of spiritual, emotional, and interpersonal growth, we will need to discuss as a group the directives found in these documents.

Finally, having passed through the stages of *forming, storming,* and *norming,* we arrive as a group at the last stage in our development: *performing.* What exactly does this stage entail? Having laid a solid foundation for life together, we are now able to live out honestly the day-to-day realities that make up our lives. Respect for other community members is cherished, and right relations among all are actively encouraged. We are able to get on, as a community, with the task at hand: living and working together.

Qualities found in a healthy religious community

With some idea of what religious communities are not and some knowledge about the stages in their development, we turn our attention now to what they can and should be. More importantly, let's examine the central place that reconciliation must hold in the life of these communities.

Today many young people have an interest in the radical possibility of adults living together in community so as to witness to reconciliation and peace.[6] Isn't that also what a religious community is meant to be? A group of adults who have come together to live fully and radically the Gospel plan as the object of their lives. What does that definition imply? That every religious community is, first and foremost, a center of spirituality and prayer. A good initial impression and lingering memory of any visitor to one of our communities should always be that he or she has been among people who pray.

What makes prayer so important in the life of a religious community? One, it has a way of transforming us. If we pray, we are better able to practice patience, withhold judgment, and love generously—some of the very qualities that foster a spirit of reconciliation. Two, prayer transforms our way of seeing reality, leaving us simpler, more humble and compassionate. All these qualities are great gifts to the life of any religious community.

Second, while a religious congregation is not a family, our family comes along with us when we join one. No, it is not present physically. But all our family taught us about self-esteem, communication, faith and spirituality, relationships, and a number of other areas accompanies us to the novitiate, and to every subsequent community in which we live.

In leaving our families to set out in life, most of us take with us some rudimentary tools we need for independent living. At the same time, we begin to realize that we are ill-equipped for many of the challenges that lie ahead. For those who come to religious life, the formation process is meant to help remedy that situation. Until very recently, however, initial formation, though it prepared us for a great deal, did very little to provide us with the necessary skills for life together in community. What are some of those skills? An ability to disagree, to comfortably give and receive affection, to speak honestly, and to extend and accept forgiveness more readily. Training in these and other competencies needed for interpersonal living merit a central place in any contemporary program of religious formation.

Third, when it comes to life in a religious community, a sense of humor is a great help. Some of us take ourselves all too seriously; we lack an ability to laugh at ourselves. How do we expect to get through life's rough spots? Humor helps us to reinterpret the meaning of some events and lessens the effect of the frustrations and reversals that are part of everyone's day-to-day existence.[7]

A sense of humor among religious is necessary for another important reason. Our way of life is meant to make people happy. That's correct: happy. Not in the sense of hilarity, but in that deep feeling of contentment experienced by people who have meaning and purpose in their life and good friends with whom to share that life.

Fourth, "active concern" toward other community members—taking the initiative and not just reacting to what others do—goes a long way toward building healthy bonds within any group of which I am a member. Noted U.S. psychologist Carl Rogers once spent a week with a friend. Each morning while out walking the two of them passed a street vendor. The friend of Rogers always greeted the man with a respectful, "Good morning." However, the vendor never responded to the greeting. Eventually, Rogers asked his friend why he persisted in saying "Good morning" to a man who plainly continued to ignore him. "Because it is the right thing to do," said his friend. "I hope that eventually he will respond as he should." The lesson was telling: the friend of Rogers was appealing to the excellence of the vendor, whether the vendor appreciated his excellence or not.[8]

Fifth, the presence of several "little virtues" among the members of any religious community goes a long way towards enhancing the group's quality of life. And what are some of those "little virtues"? Answering the door or telephone, providing a welcome to all who come calling, remembering birthdays and other special occasions, offering a word of thanks or congratulations, simply saying "hello" to those with whom I live.

An ability to celebrate is another important "little virtue" that greatly enhances community life. Ask yourself these questions. Do you enjoy being together with the other members of your community? Do you take time to celebrate together one another's birthdays and the holidays? When was the last time your community took a weekend away together solely for the enjoyment of being with one another?

Groups lacking in a spirit of celebration are hardly communities. Those who belong to them are forced eventually to look outside the group to meet most of their emotional needs. Each of the "little virtues" mentioned above doesn't cost much, but every one of them goes a long way toward creating an atmosphere in any community that makes coming home a blessing.

Life-giving communities, then, do not magically spring into existence. Their strength and success are due neither to friendship nor even a high degree of compatibility among the members of the group. While the particular mix of people in a community can make the challenge of life together more or less formidable, the presence of qualities that are life-giving in any group is the result of the hard work of its members. Similar to a good marriage or friendship, community life requires that we respect those with whom we live, make sacrifices for the common good, and work toward consensus.

We also fool ourselves when we argue that responsibility for the community's quality of life can be passed along to others in the group. Each of us has an obligation to refresh daily our commitment to those with whom we live. So, let's ask ourselves this question: what have we done lately to improve the quality of life among the members of our local community? If our answer is precious little, then surely we have a great deal of work to do.

Finally, that spirit of reconciliation with which we began our discussion needs to be at the heart of any community that calls itself religious. From time to time, one or another of us learns of a situation where the enmity between two members of a religious congregation has caused them not to speak to each other for years. Others, having suffered some injustice at the hands of a superior in time past, choose to nurture their wound, keep their anger alive, and reject any notion of reconciliation. Eventually, they become so wed to their hurt that they lose any ability to embrace the future with freedom and hope.

Evelyn and James Whitehead tell us that anger is a hedge against humiliation, a protest against the loss of self-esteem.[9] It is one thing to feel anger, though, and quite another to do something about it. With anger, as with other emotions, the goal I set for myself usually determines the action that I will take. If I want to punish you, I might insult you, or withdraw my affection and retreat into stony silence.

However, some of us, having been taught not to voice our anger, fail to express it in any helpful way. The forgiveness that so often waits on the other side of the experience gets frustrated.[10]

Reconciliation is another way of addressing our anger. It entails a process wherein we *choose* not to let the hurt we have suffered get in the way of continuing our relationship, and *decide* to respond to whoever has hurt us rather than hold on to our pain.[11] What was done is forgiven for the sake of who did it. While these decisions and choices are ours to make, cultural differences, lack of an adequate vocabulary for expressing emotional reactions, or a painful past history of managing conflict can make it more difficult for some of us to initiate the process of reconciliation. Not to do so, however, most often consigns us to the pain of our anger.

While forgiveness involves a choice and a decision, it also entails a process. Any hurt takes time to heal, trust betrayed in a relationship is rebuilt only gradually. At times, therefore, we benefit from ritualizing the process of reconciliation. Through symbol and word, in an atmosphere of prayer, we admit that our relationships are fragile, and, despite that fact, recommit ourselves to the one that was breached. The healing that results from taking such action is not limited to the persons most directly involved; reconciliation is a grace for the entire community.

Forgiveness is also a two-edged sword. There are few situations of hurt in life where only one party is to blame. In revisiting my hurt, I must also admit that I contributed to it. Thus, genuine forgiveness robs me of my hurt. I can no longer use it against you.[12]

Are there some disappointments and hurts in life that are impossible to heal? Not if we are open to God's grace and willing to take the time to be reconciled. In all of this, we do well to remember the Lord's directive about forgiving seventy times seven. Understanding more fully the message of that Gospel lesson, we can better appreciate the wisdom that the old rabbi was passing along to his students. Yes, we will know when the night has ended and the day is returning.

Reconciliation, reminding us of our weakness, helps nurture in us a compassionate and loving heart. Such a heart is necessary if we are to be able to look on the face of any person in community and see that woman or man as our sister or brother. In gradually developing that capacity, we come to know full well that regardless of the time, it is no longer night for us.

Reflection Questions

1. What do you look for in a religious community?
2. What has been your experience of community life to date? Are there skills that you wish you had or could learn that would make community life more rewarding for you? What can you do in a practical way to acquire those skills?

Notes

[1] John Malich, FMS, *Community: Life Giving or Stagnant* (Canfield, OH: Alba House Cassettes, 1997).

[2] Wittberg, *Creating a Future for Religious Life,* 3-4.

[3] Ibid.

[4] Ibid.

[5] Irvin D. Yalom, *Theory and Practice of Group Therapy* (New York, NY: Basic Books, 1995).

[6] Osiek, "A woman stands at Mount Nebo."

[7] Evelyn Eaton Whitehead and James D. Whitehead, *Seasons of Strength: New Visions of Christian Maturing* (Garden City, NY: Doubleday, 1984), 124-125.

[8] John Johnston, FSC, *Look to the Future: Build Communities Today that are Innovative, Creative and Holy* (Rome: Tipografia S.G.S., 1998), 63.

[9] Whitehead and Whitehead, *Seasons of Strength,* 117-127.

[10] Ibid.

[11] Ibid.

[12] Ibid.

Chapter VI

SPIRITUALITY: TURN ON YOUR HEART LIGHTS

"I learned many years ago," wrote Joseph Bernardin some weeks before he died, "that the only way I could give quality time to prayer was by getting up early in the morning. The early hours of the morning, before the phones and doorbells started to ring, before the mail arrived, seemed to me to be the best for spending quality time with the Lord. So I promised God and myself that I would give the first hour of each day to prayer."[1]

After telling his readers that he had been faithful to his promise for more than 20 years, Bernardin went on to make two points. First of all, he admitted that he had not learned to pray perfectly. Like all of us, he had to contend with distractions and preoccupations about the problems he would face during the day just getting underway.

Second, early on he made another decision. He said, "Lord, I know I spend a certain amount of that morning hour of prayer daydreaming, problem-solving, and I'm not sure that I can cut that out. I'll try, but the important thing is, I'm not going to give that time to anybody else. So even though it may not unite me as much with you as it should, nobody else is going to get that time."[2]

The Cardinal brought his reflection to a close by explaining just what he did with that hour of prayer each day. He prayed some of the *Liturgy of the Hours* with the belief that it united him with others who daily pray this prayer. He also often prayed the rosary and reported that it provided him with vivid images of the Lord's life, and of Mary's also. Finally, he spent time in mental prayer and reflection, nourishing both with the words of Scripture and good books about spirituality.

The way we were

A number of spiritual writers would be pleased to read about Joseph Bernardin's morning prayer routine. Throughout the ages, they have prescribed some of the same time-honored practices to help us sustain ourselves in our chosen way of life. Regular private and communal prayer, Eucharist, frequent reception of the sacrament of reconciliation, the practice of charity and self-sacrifice, life in community, obedience to those entrusted with leadership in the congregation, ministry and concrete involvement with the poor, and a willingness to be vulnerable, as Jesus was vulnerable—all have been recommended as suitable means for developing a spiritual life.[3] To this list, each of our religious congregations has usually added some ritual practices of its own. Careful observance of this array of prayers, sacraments, and acts of charity was seen as the way to persevere. Religious relied on these means and others, such as an annual retreat, to sustain them over time in their commitment.

The practices outlined above, realized in fresh and cogent ways, are still good means by which to nourish ourselves spiritually. However, today we must also ask if something additional is needed. After all, the world of faith has changed dramatically since Vatican II. We are living during an age called post-modernity, and have become aware of the world's growing need for a new and compelling image of God. The God of the past, so often called on to fill in gaps for weaknesses found in science, no longer makes sense to most of us.[4]

We also realize that the world in which we live can no longer be expected to carry the faith for us. The time is long past when we could count on living in a Christian culture, or even on being surrounded by people of faith.[5] Sad to say, in some religious communities today, those who wish to have a vibrant life of faith cannot always count on others in their group for support.[6]

Over a quarter century ago, spiritual writer Henri Nouwen made an observation that helps provide a perspective on the challenges we face today in the areas of prayer and spirituality. Nouwen remarked that believing in the idea of Christianity, or a code of ethics, or the human value of gathering as a community, or God's call for justice, is, for some of us, easier than having personal faith in a living God. On what evidence did he base this observation? During an age characterized as secular and seductive, God apparently no longer had a place in the personal lives of many of the Yale University seminarians that Nouwen was teaching at the time.[7]

What kind of God do we long for today? One who will dwell at the center of our lives, a God who will provide depth of meaning and an answer to our ultimate concerns.[8] This is the God around whom we must begin to build a new spirituality and a life of personal and communal prayer. That life of prayer must be true to the ideals of our characteristic and distinctive way of living out the Gospel message, the charisms and traditions of our respective congregations, and the unique elements found in our culture.

Are U.S. religious praying?

The vast majority of U.S. religious pray and, by their own report, they pray regularly.[9] So, any recent rumors about a lack of a spirit of prayer among men and women religious in the States appear unfounded. Women religious report a greater commitment to prayer than do religious priests or brothers. Those called to contemplative life rate common prayer, the sacrament of reconciliation, devotion to Mary, and the opportunity for an annual retreat as very important to their sense of personal and spiritual fulfillment. Older religious value prayer more and experience greater satisfaction with it than do their younger sisters or brothers in consecrated life. Without any doubt, however, contemporary religious in the U.S.—young and old—are praying.[10]

With that said, we must also admit that we face several challenges today in the area of prayer. A profound and loving relationship with God is the foundation upon which our life together is built. However, the specific forms in which that relationship is to be expressed and celebrated are often a topic of considerable discussion and, at times, disagreement. Some of us, members of apostolic congregations, find ourselves unable to be faithful to a prescribed schedule of common prayer more suited to the rhythm of the monastery than to the day-to-day demands made on active religious.

For others, the form that our community's common prayer will take continues to be a source of tension. Differences in age, life experience, formation, personality, and images of God often interfere with our group's ability to reach consensus in this area. For still others of us, Eucharist—at its best a sign of unity—is instead a painful source of conflict. Let's admit it: to raise the issue of common prayer and its place in the transformation of religious life in the U.S. today, and at the same time avoid the obstacle to communion that some women religious experience as they approach the eucharistic celebration, is simply not possible anymore.[11]

Spirituality

The challenges that we face in our life of prayer fall properly under the heading of *spirituality*. Before going any farther, though, let's be clear about the meaning of that word. Theologian Ronald Rolheiser, OMI suggests that spirituality has more to do with the unquenchable fire that burns within each of us than with pious practices. In his view, growth in the spiritual life is, more than anything else, a process of creatively disciplining the fiery energy—or passion—that flows through us.[12] And what gives us the courage to undertake this task? The fact that our hunger and thirst for God far exceeds our pride, our selfishness and our greed.[13]

Many of us claim to possess passion enough for two or three lifetimes! And we have little trouble admitting that this driving force, lying at the center of our human experience, is the source of the love, creativity, and hope that we bring to life.[14]

But passion has more than one face. More often than not, it appears in the form of unbridled longing or desire and we describe it as a hunger, an unquenchable flame, or a wildness that cannot be tamed.[15] This face of our passion leaves us restless, dissatisfied, and frustrated. And, in the midst of all this unrest, just what is spirituality? Ultimately, it's what we do with our passion.[16]

This approach to spirituality is not what most of us were taught during our early years, and well into adulthood. We got off to a false start because we were led to believe that to be fit for God, we had to painstakingly ascend a ladder of virtues.[17] But any relationship with Jesus comes at his initiative, not ours. The saints and mystics in Church history came to accept eventually Jesus' great love for each of them. Teresa of Avila, for example, often said that when she lacked the words for prayer, she went into her convent chapel and sat before the Blessed Sacrament, so that the Lord could look on her with love. Unlike Teresa, few of us appear willing to believe that God loves us in such an unconditional way.

But our hunger for Jesus is nothing more than a reflection of his for us. So, why try to tame God's love by pretending that something given so freely must be earned? Or, to trivialize it by celebrating empty rituals? In this life we have little choice but to bear tensions that cannot be relieved, and to live with longings that cannot be fulfilled. Nothing but ourselves, however, stands in the way of our accepting Jesus' unconditional love.

Spirituality and sexuality

We have evidence enough, then, that desire and longing, what we have been calling passion, play an important role in our spiritual life. But passion's power is ambitious. It also appears to be at work in other areas of our life where strong emotions hold sway. For example, whenever we experience anger and rage, passion is close at hand. So, too, in situations of profound sadness and ecstatic joy. Why be surprised, then, with the suggestion that passion holds a place of prominence in our sexual lives?[18]

At this point, you might find yourself wondering: aren't we going far afield from the topic of this chapter? After all, didn't it begin with a discussion about prayer and spirituality? So, let's quickly clear up the matter before us and, with answer in hand, get back to our task. Is there a relationship between our spiritual lives and our sexuality? Quite simply: yes. Rolheiser not only suggests that spirituality and sexuality are closely related, he goes so far as to say that sexuality—this positive, but also most powerful and dangerous of all the fires that burn within us—lies at the heart of any life worth calling spiritual.[19]

But what does the word *sexuality* imply? Surely something more than genital sex. Its Latin root, *secare,* means to be cut off or severed from the whole. And isn't that our experience in life? From our earliest days, we feel incomplete and lonely, and long for some kind of union. Well before the genital sexual awakening that comes with puberty, don't we find ourselves reaching out to others in friendship?

With the passage of time we also begin to realize that sexual and spiritual energy are more closely related than we first imagined. Both, we discover, have the same end: union with others and with the Other. These two passions of ours are friends, not foes. They draw us out of ourselves and into relationships.

But similar to spirituality, sexuality wears more than one face. While it gives us a zest for living, contributes to romance in a relationship, and is the source of unusual courage and heroic generosity, this very same energy also can lead us into self-destructive and de-humanizing behavior. On those occasions when we lose our sense of balance, sexuality contributes to our running about and out of control. With what long-term results? We either die from an overdose of life, or we lose our zest for living it.[20]

Are means available to help us channel our sexual longing and desire in creative ways, ways that lead us away from self-defeating behavior and toward union with God and others? Actually there are several. A sense of discipline, a capacity for honest self-appraisal, an ability to tolerate solitude, and a sense of humor.

For centuries now, spiritual directors have recommended these same tools to men and women with a serious interest in their religious growth. And their recommendation stands to reason. After all, our degree of integration in body, mind and spirit depends, to a large extent, upon the disciplines and habits by which we choose to live. The quality of our relationships with God, others, our world, and ourselves also is influenced by these very same choices.[21]

What is our challenge, then, when it comes to sexuality and spirituality? To become friends with the passion within us and, at the same time, accept the fact that all symphonies in life are unfinished. Though our culture teaches us otherwise, we cannot have it all. We are naïve to believe that we can be fulfilled completely in this life. We must, instead, learn to live with tension in both our spiritual and sexual lives. Augustine was right: our hearts remain restless until they rest fully in God.

Spirituality and celibate chastity

If sexuality lies at the center of the spiritual life, the spiritual life is likewise at the heart of genuine celibate chaste living. As men and women religious, we can learn all there is to know about human sexuality, but if we fail to take on the identity of a religious person, we shall always be ill at ease with our celibate chastity. To be at home with our choice for celibate chastity, then, we have to face—first and foremost—what it means to be a religious person.

And what does that task require? To begin with, that we accept the fact that Jesus is the answer to the question that is at the heart of every human life.[22] Consequently, my relationship with him rests at the center of my life. And concretely that means putting aside time to nurture this relationship, and allowing Jesus to be himself. Healthy relationships foster the freedom of all involved. My relationship with Jesus should be no different.

Jesuit Thomas Green uses the image of a well to illustrate this last point.[23] He compares the consoling grace found in our relationship with Jesus to water bubbling to the surface of a well, almost to the point of overflowing. Early in our relationship with the Lord, we are young and strong and can easily draw water from the well. We have available to us as much of God's consoling grace as we desire. But we are in charge, not Jesus.

With the passage of time the water level in the well begins to drop. But we still have our strength, and so, with human effort, we continue to lower a bucket into the well and draw forth as much consoling grace as we like. But we remain in control. Jesus continues to be kept at a distance.

Eventually, however, that well, once brimming with water, dries up. And no longer young and strong, we lack the self-sufficiency of our earlier years. So, we ask ourselves: what can we do now to gain the consoling grace of God? An honest response: nothing, except to sit and wait for the rain.

When we arrive at this point in our spiritual life, we are better able to allow Jesus to be at least an equal partner in our relationship. We give him the freedom to love us as he sees fit. And how do we know that we are moving in this direction? When, like Teresa, we long only for a simple presence before God. Nothing more, and nothing less.

The second characteristic of a religious person builds upon the first: we accept the fact that Jesus loves us in a singular and special way. From the beginning of time, God has reached out to us in relationship, with Jesus being the most stunning example of that initiative. Every friendship that we have in life develops in a distinct and unrepeatable manner. So, too, our relationship with Jesus and its pattern of development are unique. They cannot be duplicated. Everyone's spirituality must be tailor-made to reflect these realities.

Unfortunately, throughout life many of us are presented with formulas and plans of action that carry with them some guarantee of success in the spiritual life but, unfortunately, fail to respect the unique relationship that we have with Jesus. Rather than enhancing that relationship, a number of these methods only get in the way.

Third, to be a religious person we need to remain open to the spiritual awakenings that take place in our lives, and to be willing to explore the longing and desire that are so much a part of each of them. During the adolescent years, most of us experience a sexual awakening. Powerful sexual feelings, genital desire, and a feeling of urgency mark it.

A spiritual awakening is similar. When our natural spirituality wakes up, intense spiritual desire begins to emerge. The process can be dramatic, as in a conversion experience, or—as is more common—gradual. When the latter occurs, we notice that, over time, our desire for God begins to grow.

Finally, as a religious person we accept the fact that we don't have to do anything to be worthy of God's love. It is given freely to us with no strings attached. We can say "yes" to it or reject it, but the idea of having to earn God's love is just out of the question. This last quality of a religious person is the most difficult for most of us to accept. And why is this so? In part, because we are embarrassed by God's unrestrained passion for us.

A great deal more can be said about spirituality, sexuality, and celibate chastity. But these topics are not the focus of this book. Readers with an interest in learning more about any of these three are referred to one of several references listed in the endnotes for this chapter.

Spiritual growth

We pay a price when getting involved with Jesus on his terms. After all, he asks us to imitate him, not admire him. And that means embracing the Paschal Mystery. If we seek transformation, we must first learn to be at home with suffering and death.

How does any relationship with Jesus develop, and what is needed to sustain it? To begin with, throughout the ages, spiritual writers have insisted that times of personal prayer are an essential part of any relationship with the Lord. And for that bond to deepen, these moments of prayer must eventually grow to be regular and prolonged. What does the phrase "regular and prolonged period" mean concretely? Ideally, an hour each day.

You and I have the pleasure of Jesus' company twenty-four hours a day, seven days a week. If we are serious about our relationship with him, we will want to return the favor by providing Jesus with the pleasure of our company for at least one hour each day. This time-honored practice and integrity in our moral life are two elements found among people who take their spiritual life seriously.

Those of us who are members of apostolic religious congregations may balk at the idea of trying to find another uninterrupted hour for personal prayer in the midst of an already busy day. So we ask defensively: "Aren't those with a call to monastic or contemplative life better able to respond courageously to the challenge of finding an 'extended period' for prayer each day? Jesus realizes that I am burdened already with a busy apostolic life; he will understand. So much remains to be done, and already there are hardly sufficient hours in the day to accomplish my tasks."

The *busyness* that marks the lives of many of us in religious life today borders on the pathological. For some of us, it is the single greatest threat to our interior life. For what reason? Rolheiser calls to our attention three spirit-numbing elements that lie at the heart of this type of busyness: narcissism, pragmatism, and unbridled restlessness.[24]

Narcissistic people are excessively self-preoccupied. While

121

any spirituality can become overly privatized—a "Jesus and I" cult of self-indulgence—the narcissism of overly busy people gives rise to just the opposite problem: a lack of sufficient interiority to sustain any significant degree of intimacy with the Lord.[25] Confronted with their need to depend radically upon God, narcissistic men and women are unable to achieve the required self-surrender. When it comes to the spiritual life, narcissists entertain this delusion: their work is their prayer.

Pragmatism is a second enemy of the interior life. Preoccupied with efficiency, pragmatic people focus almost exclusively on work, achievement, and life's practical concerns.[26]

Unbridled restlessness is a third foe of our spiritual life. Those of us who suffer from this malady greedily seek out one experience after another. Educator Neil Postman describes this state of affairs as "amusing oneself to death."[27] Unfortunately, the distraction that unbridled restlessness introduces into our lives interferes with our ability to develop a spirit of solitude, so necessary for a genuine prayer life.

In contrast, in the lives of those who pray regularly and in the life of their congregation, the fruits and gifts of the Holy Spirit are evident. Numbered among those fruits are charity, a spirit of joy, patience, forbearance, faith, and reverence for oneself and others. Among the gifts: wisdom, understanding, counsel, knowledge, piety, fortitude, and fear of the Lord. As we look at our lives and the lives of our group today, let's ask ourselves first, are the fruits and gifts of the Spirit present? If so, how are they working together for the renewal of our institutes? What if we find them wanting in our own lives or that of our congregation? Then we need to wonder about how seriously we take our relationship with Jesus. More importantly, we must decide which aspects of our lives we must change in order to bring our practice into line with what we espouse publicly.

Christianity is not just another philosophy of life, nor can it be reduced simply to a moral code.[28] No, our Christian life, at its heart, is all about a relationship with Jesus. That relationship is the solution for our restiveness. It is also the place where any lasting renewal of religious life and of our prayer life must begin.

Additional aids to prayer

In addition to embracing the Paschal Mystery and the twin supports of personal prayer and integrity in our moral life, what other practices did Jesus prescribe to insure a healthy spiritual life? Three come to mind. One, a passion for justice; two, a grateful heart; three, concrete involvement within a historical community of faith.[29]

Why be surprised that involvement in creating justice for the poor is an essential element of the spiritual life? For Jesus, there were two basic commandments: love God, and love your neighbor. In spelling out their details, he bluntly tells us that we will be judged on how we treat people who are poor. The way in which we treat them will be equated to the way in which we treat God.

We are kidding ourselves if we think we can relate to God without also continually looking at how the weakest members in our society are faring and how our own lifestyle is contributing to their plight. Genuine spirituality cannot be cut off from persons who are poor and their concerns, and the need for a just society.[30]

A grateful heart is another important element in the spiritual life. After all, to be a saint is to be fueled by gratitude.[31] It stands to reason, then, that only grateful hearts will ever be able to transform our world spiritually. The tale of the Prodigal Son illustrates this last point. Both sons are "away from their father's house"; one through infidelity and weakness, the other due to bitterness and anger.

Either son was entitled to his inheritance, even while his father was alive. But the latter, for as long as he lived, was to be guaranteed the interest gained on any assets transferred to one or another of his sons. In taking his inheritance and moving to a foreign land, the younger son denied his father his due interest. He sinned, not so much because of his loose living in a foreign land, but because he figuratively wished his father dead.[32]

But his older brother was no better. Yes, he did all the right things, but for all the wrong reasons. There was no celebration in his heart. Jesus asks us to avoid imitating either son and, instead, encourages us to look to the grateful heart of the father and to take on his compassion.[33]

Finally, spirituality has both an individual and a community focus. God calls us not only as particular persons but also as a group.[34] Some of us find that fact hard to accept. We want God but we don't want institutions such as the Church. Its humanity and its sinfulness embarrass us. The search for the face of God must have a communal dimension; it can never be solely an individual quest. We also do well to remember that we are part of our all too human and sinful Church, the one that is so often the object of our criticism.

Common prayer

When the members of a religious community come together to plan their life of common prayer, their first question should not be: What time in the morning and evening should we come together to pray? Instead, these more fundamental questions merit primary attention: Just how do we want to praise God as a group?

How best celebrate as a community our hunger and thirst for Jesus? To arrive at a satisfying answer, we need to have some knowledge in three areas: the evolution of common prayer in religious life from the Age of the Desert up until the present time; two, those elements that make up our unique U.S. approach to spirituality; and three, an understanding of just how the structure of our own congregation's community prayer developed.

Perhaps you find yourself uneasy as you read this suggested approach to the question of common prayer. Using this method for organizing community prayer gives rise to the possibility that each community of a given congregation may arrive at a different style and format for common prayer. Should that happen, what would be the outcome? Hopefully, in a given congregations each community's common prayer would be more in keeping with its members' image of God, the reality of their day-to-day lives and ministries, and consonant with the rich spiritual traditions of their Institute.

Let's now take a look at how, down through history, different forms of common prayer developed in consecrated life and, more importantly, the factors that gave rise to those changes.

A brief history of common prayer

Both the form and frequency of common prayer within consecrated life have been shaped by the concrete reality of the lives of religious at a given time in history. Often enough, the catalyst for the evolution of common prayer was either one or another development in the Church at large or time constraints arising from ministry. Painting in broad strokes for a moment, the Benedictine communities of the Middle Ages were partial to the Divine Office. It consisted of the chanting of psalms, interspersed with readings from the Fathers of the Church.[35]

By the 10th and 11th centuries, however, the Eucharist—now elevated to a position of supreme importance among all the prayers of the Church—had usurped the Divine Office's privileged position and taken its place at the center of the monastic day.[36]

Appearing on the scene during the high Middle Ages, the Cistercians and Beguines were quite revolutionary in their approach to personal and common prayer and to spirituality. They emphasized the intention behind formal prayers. Their "affective mysticism" eventually included a number of mystical validations of prayer—levitations, trances, the stigmata, and so forth.

By the 16th century, Ignatius of Loyola had come along and developed new techniques for structured meditations on the life of Christ and the great truths of the faith. His contribution led to changes in the type of prayer practiced by the members of many religious congregations. Rather than emphasize the recitation of the Divine Office or mystical contemplation, Ignatius directed his Jesuit confreres to perform the "Spiritual Exercises" during their annual retreat, these Exercises being founded on discursive meditation. The three powers of memory, intellect, and will were all to be used.[37]

These new practices became quite popular among the members of a number of congregations. Many groups founded in the 19th century adopted Ignatius's recommendation of an annual retreat and made meditation the basis of their community prayer style.[38] The affective mysticism of the Cistercians and the Beguines, so popular in the 12th and 13th centuries, was put aside in favor of structured reflections on pre-selected points or topics. This type of mental prayer was taught in many novitiates in the U.S. until shortly after Vatican II.

With the coming of the 19th century, however, many of the new congregations discarded the Divine Office as the community's prayer. They substituted, instead, a series of devotional prayers—novenas, rosaries, morning and evening prayers, litanies, etc. These practices mirrored what was happening at the time in the larger Catholic culture. Why abandon the Divine Office in favor of all these devotional practices? Because recitation of all the hours of the Office interfered with the teaching or nursing duties of the men and women who made up the congregations that had recently come into existence.[39]

In time, as we can see, the mystical, contemplative prayer—or affective mysticism—that Bernard of Clairvaux had recommended as a matter of course fell into disuse and those who aspired to it were judged to be arrogant and even dangerous. Thelma Hall, RC, a well-known spiritual director, points out that for the last two to three centuries contemplation has been under a cloud.[40] It was judged to be appropriate only for a small group of the spiritually elite. This mistaken notion has managed to impoverish our entire Church. Men and women religious from apostolic congregations have been especially perplexed. Though told by many that they are called to be contemplatives in action, one of the essential ingredients of that model—contemplation—has, until recently, been denied them.

The style and form of common prayer within religious congregations, then, has evolved over time, drawing freely from the many new forms of prayer that developed during one or another periods in Church history.[41] Today, as we re-examine our spiritualities and fashion anew our common prayers, recalling the history of community prayer is an essential exercise. So also is taking measure of the many innovative styles and forms of praying that are developing in new prayer movements springing up within the Catholic communion and in other Christian churches.

A world Church

In addition to understanding factors that influenced the evolution of common prayer over the history of consecrated life, some knowledge of developments in our Church as a whole can be of help as we shape the form and frequency of common prayer in religious life in the States today. The late Jesuit theologian Karl Rahner, during a brief address at the Weston School of Theology in 1978, identified three stages in the history of our Church. First of all, he observed, we passed through the very short period of Jewish Christianity. Jerusalem was the Church's center and its life was dominated by the resurrection of Jesus.[42]

Paul can be held responsible for the second stage in the history of our Church: the period of western Christianity. Some startling changes took place as our Church moved from one of Jewish Christianity to one dominated by western ways of thinking. The observant Jewish Christian, for example, saw circumcision declared unnecessary for non-Jews. The Sabbath was abolished and the Church's center moved to Rome. Paul and his associates faced a formidable dilemma: what to preserve from the world of Jewish Christianity, Jewish law, and Old Testament salvation history.

In time, Christianity spread out from Europe to many parts of the then known world. Roman-Hellenist ways of thinking influenced Christianity's form, as did Europe's 16th century colonialism and imperialism. For example: Latin was exported to countries where it had no previous history, and Roman law was promulgated via canon law. The religious experience of people of other cultures was often rejected and western morality was imposed on all who made up the then known world.

Today, however, the phenomenon of globalization is helping a world Church to be born. Rapid forms of transport, widespread migration, and a revolution in communications have reduced distances between countries, their peoples and cultures. Consequently, our Church is being challenged to shed its predominantly western mindset and to forge a new synthesis between communion and theological diversity, and between spirituality and life experience. The Church's reaction to these developments? Often enough, resistance at the center to change. Such a response is unfortunate. Why? Because, to the extent that our Church remains predominantly western, it will never really be catholic.

A unique U.S. spirituality

Are we as U.S. Catholics different from our counterparts in other parts of the world? Apparently so and, really, to the surprise of no one. For example, even as our Church and religious life were being established in North America, rather harsh judgments—on the part of European superiors—weighed in against those born on this continent who were entering congregations. Emigrating from France, Bishop Dubourg of Saint Louis, and Mother Theodore Guerin, who established the Sisters of Providence in the U.S., looked with suspicion on certain character traits found among people born in this new land. The prevalent cult of freedom found among these people versus what, in Dubourg and Guerin's view, was the discipline found among Europeans, and the spirit of equality evident in the U.S. versus the hierarchical system in which Europe was entrenched were particularly troubling to the two of them.[43]

People from Europe were not alone in their suspicion. Bishop John Carroll of Baltimore wrote that the idea of affiliating Mother Seton's Institute with the French *Filles de la charité* failed due to the different character of both countries.[44] Many of these differences had their roots in the process of inculturation that

129

had taken place in the young nation. Independence produced among the citizens of the new country a strong tendency to differentiate themselves from the "old world." John Quincy Adams, then Secretary of State, admonished a German baron that immigrants must "cast off the European skin, never to resume it."[45]

Similar sentiments were to be found in some American-born religious leaders like Isaac Hecker, and later even some European-born churchmen, such as John Ireland, who came to dislike the foreign flavor that the Catholic Church was taking on in the States. Over time this development became increasingly obvious: a common historical experience in what many saw as a "new world" was helping to shape the life and way of thinking of U.S. religious.

The heart of the matter

So, the power of a ghetto-like socio-cultural world transplanted from Europe and initially quite influential in shaping the attitudes and way of life of U.S. religious began eventually to weaken. With what consequences? Features more typical of an American approach to spirituality became increasingly evident in the lives of sisters, brothers, and religious priests.[46] The traditional view of God, for example, came to be a gracious giver, and the traditional dualisms of nature/grace and spirit/body were surpassed in favor of a tendency toward synthesis.

Other qualities, typical of our national character, also became more apparent in our approach to spirituality and in our prayer life. Our respect for freedom and a strong sense of basic equality grew in importance, as did our pronounced love of nature and communion with it. We became ever more sensitive to issues of social justice and organized against any forms of discrimination.

Being a pragmatic people, we tended to emphasize the apostolic aspects of our life over the contemplative. Our sensitivity to what experience has to teach us served to remind us that the Spirit works also through individuals, groups, and the national character of the country.

Finally, the pluralistic nature of our society helped us to practice tolerance. In time, it was evident that we had greater openness to other believers and to other religions than did many of our European counterparts.

Spirituality and prayer

We face some formidable challenges today as we work to create new forms and styles of common prayer for consecrated life in the U.S. As mentioned earlier, we need to be conscious of the ways in which community prayer in consecrated life has evolved over the centuries. We also have to be sensitive to the influence of our distinctly American ways of looking at our world. There are, however, some other very practical obstacles that we must overcome if we are to address our task adequately.

For example, how often do you and the members of your local community talk about spirituality? Better yet, with what frequency do you share with others in the group your experience of Jesus, your struggles in prayer, the hopes and joys that you bring before the Lord? For most of us, the answer to our first question is "rarely." To the second? Some of us might not be able to recall even one occasion where we shared our personal experience of spirituality with those with whom we lived in community.

What makes frank talk about spirituality so difficult? We have pointed out already that factors such as temperament and formation no doubt play a role. For at least some of us, they are

131

the troublesome sources of our inhibition. Lack of an adequate vocabulary with which to describe our spiritual life can be another stumbling block. Young people with an interest in religious life, however, are increasingly perplexed by the inability or unwillingness of many of us in religious life to talk freely about Jesus. After all, they ask, isn't religious life primarily all about Jesus and the reign of God?

Lack of knowledge of our congregation's history when it comes to common prayer is another obstacle that gets in the way of some free exchange about the subject, and its structure and place in our lives as apostolic religious. In my Institute, for example, our traditional morning prayer includes, along with the *Prayer of Christians* and a number of devotional prayers, the *Salve Regina* and a series of invocations to saints, prophets, angels, and archangels. Like every congregation's community prayer, that of my own has a history. The *Salve*, for example, was added in 1830, thirteen years after the group's foundation and during the time of the "second" French Revolution. Saint Marcellin Champagnat, our founder, had great devotion to Mary. He added the *Salve* to morning and evening prayer to ask Mary to protect his young community and its members during a time of civil strife.

Our first Superior General, Brother François, added the invocations that we recite each morning. He was concerned about a safe journey for the young brothers who had been sent out from France to establish the Institute in South Africa.[47] That province celebrated its 100th anniversary several years ago, so presumably the brothers arrived without a mishap! However, the invocations recited so fervently by their contemporaries to insure their safe passage continue to be part of our community prayer today. Some knowledge about the developmental history of common prayer in our own congregation obviously can save us from rigidly holding on to forms and styles of worship that were appropriate for one time in history but are less than adequate for the group's needs today.

Spirituality, manifest in personal and common prayer, is at the heart of our lives as religious. Without both, we soon drift away from the ideals of consecrated life. Regular and sustained personal prayer must be the well from which we refresh ourselves daily. The relationship that we have with Jesus is a sure and steady source of strength and enthusiasm.

Common prayer is equally important. To fashion it in new forms, however, we must take the risk of saying something to the other members of the community about our relationship with God in personal prayer. Sharing the thrill of that adventure with the other members of our congregation will insure that together we will find new and satisfying ways of praising God, ways in keeping with new forms of religious life in this country that are in the making.

In addition, we must also be true to the charism of our foundress or founder. And we must respect our history as a people and nation, new insights into the spiritual life, the voices of the young, and the traditions and customs of our Church groups.

Jesus provides us with a helpful model of creativity when it comes to formulating new styles and forms of prayer and praise of God. Faced with a disciple's request for instruction in prayer, the Lord—in fashioning his response—drew on his own experience of personal prayer, and showed sensitivity to issues of culture, prayer forms of the Jewish people of his day, and his mission. And so he responded, "When you pray, say this: Father, holy is your name...." And to no one's surprise, all understood the language of prayer that he spoke.

Reflection Questions

1. The members of your local community agree to put aside a day to discuss the group's common prayer. What contributions do you plan to make to the discussion?

2. What is your initial reaction to this statement: An hour of personal prayer each day should, more often than not, be the norm for members of apostolic religious congregations?

   If you agree with this statement, what adjustments might you need to make personally in your life to assure an hour a day for personal prayer?

Notes

1. Joseph Cardinal Bernardin, *The Gift of Peace* (London: Darton, Longman and Todd, 1998), 96-100.
2. Ibid.
3. Ronald Rolheiser, "A spirituality for our time," *LCWR Occasional Papers* (Fall 1999), 1-18.
4. Ibid.
5. Ibid.
6. Ibid.
7. Henri Nouwen, *Intimacy: Essays in Pastoral Psychology* (San Francisco, CA: Harper and Row, 1969).
8. Ronald Rolheiser, "A spirituality for our time," 11-18.
9. Nygren and Ukeritis, *The Future of Religious Orders in the United States,* 177-180.
10. Ibid.
11. Mary Collins, OSB, "Is the Eucharist Still a Source of Meaning for Women?" in Paul Philibert, OP, ed., *Living in the Meantime* (Mahwah, NJ: Paulist, 1994), 185-196.
12. This section on spirituality and those that follow immediately draw heavily on the work of Ronald Rolheiser, *The Holy Longing: The Search for a Christian Spirituality.* (New York, NY: Doubleday, 1999), 3-19.
13. Radcliffe, *Sing a New Song,* 28.
14. Rolheiser, *The Holy Longing,* 4-5.
15. Ibid., 3-19.
16. Ibid.
17. Ibid.

18 See Seán Sammon, *An Undivided Heart: Making Sense of Celibate Chastity* (Staten Island, NY: Alba House, 1993). Also, Rolheiser, *The Holy Longing,* 192-212.

19 Ronald Rolheiser, *The Holy Longing,* 192-212.

20 Ibid., 8.

21 Ibid., 11.

22 George Weigel, "Spiritual Stars of the Millennium: 51," *The Tablet* 23/30, December 2000, 1781.

23 Thomas Green, *Drinking from a Dry Well* (Notre Dame, IN: Ave Maria Press, 1991).

24 Rolheiser, *The Holy Longing,* 32.

25 Ibid.

26 Ibid.

27 Neil Postman, *Amusing Ourselves to Death: Public Discourse in the Age of Show Business* (New York: Penguin Books, 1985).

28 Rolheiser, *The Holy Longing,* 63.

29 Ibid., 53-70.

30 Ibid.

31 Ibid.

32 Henri J.M. Nouwen, *The Return of the Prodigal Son: A Story of Homecoming* (London: Darton, Longman, and Todd, 1992), 34-44.

33 Rolheiser, *The Holy Longing,* 68-69.

34 Wittberg, *The Rise and Fall of Catholic Religious Orders,* 128.

35 Ibid.

36 Ibid., 129.

37 Ibid.

38 Ibid.

39 Ibid., 130.

40 Thelma Hall, RC, *Too Deep for Words: Rediscovering the Lectio Divina* (Mahwah, NJ: Paulist Press, 1988).

41 John Manuel Lozano, "Religious Life: The Continuing Journey... Vision and Hope," 143-161.

42 Karl Rahner, "Toward a Fundamental Theological Interpretation of Vatican II," *Theological Studies* 40:4 (December 1979).

43 Ibid.

44 Quoted by Annabelle M. Melville, *John Carroll of Baltimore* (New York, NY: Scribner, 1955), 162.

45 Lozano, "Religious Life: The Continuing Journey... Vision and Hope," 150.

46 Ibid., 152.

47 Personal communication, Brother Jude Pieterse, FMS, April 2000.

Chapter VII

FRESH FACES
AT THE
BREAKFAST
TABLE[1]

In April 1997 the murder in New York of Jonathan Levin, a 31-year-old schoolteacher, captured the attention of the people of that city. From the discovery of his body in a modest Upper West Side apartment until the apprehension of two suspects, not a day passed without the newspapers carrying one or more stories about this generous young man.

Some believed that Levin's murder might have escaped public attention had he not been the son of Time-Warner's chief executive officer. Be that as it may, the simple fact remains that here was a son of privilege who had chosen to serve the children of poverty. Levin taught at Taft High School, located in a violent and economically depressed area of the Bronx.

Here was a man who, loving poetry and literature, passed along that passion to young people whose lives are so often devoid of beauty. He stirred in more than a few of them a desire to put pen to paper and write. Yes, he sowed the virtue of hope among those who had almost ceased to believe in themselves.

What was it about the life and death of Jonathan Levin that caught the attention of so many? Was it that he came from wealth but lived simply and frugally? Was it merely that he was a young man in a profession that had fallen from grace in the U.S. in recent years? Or was it his willingness to go that extra mile with those he taught?

Perhaps Levin was so attractive to a large number of people for a very different reason. Having discovered his life's dream, this young man had chosen to live it out fully. Not a simple nor an easy task, and one that called for sacrifice. But, with what results? A life filled with purpose and meaning.

Why tell the story of this young man and his dream? More to the point, what do his life and death have to do with the challenge of vocation promotion today? The answer is simple: vocation promotion is all about uncovering dreams—in our lives and in the lives of others. Without doubt, a great deal of fine work encouraging vocations is underway at the moment within a number of religious congregations in the States. We need to acknowledge that fact and commend those involved. However, we also need to admit that many of us appear to have forgotten how to carry out this important task: helping young men and women to discover and develop the dream that God has in mind for them and for their lives.

Two vocation tales

How serious a problem is the challenge of vocation promotion among religious in the United States? Quite serious. The stories of two young men, Tim and Sean, illustrate but one aspect of the dilemma: our current failure to invite young people to join our congregations.

I first met Tim, a young man in his early 30's, when I visited the formation house where he was a novice. More than a decade earlier, Tim had attended a high school owned, administered, and generously staffed by a congregation of religious brothers. During the years that Tim was a student, at any one time about 25 members of this group served at the school.

Another congregation of men religious also worked at Tim's school. However, this group had but three of their members serving on the school's faculty.

In Tim's last year of high school he made a decision to join this second congregation. He remained with them for a year, but subsequently left them, finished college, and got a job and worked for several years.

About two years prior to our meeting, Tim had contacted a member of the community that owned and administered his high school to talk about joining this group's formation program. On hearing his story, I wondered what had motivated Tim to enter the congregation that he did after secondary school, leave them about a year later, and then several years afterwards join the formation program of the congregation of which he was now a member. So I asked him, "What made you enter another Order 12 years ago?"

"It's really quite simple," he told me. "They asked me to join." Tim then went on to say that he had always wanted to be a member of the congregation in which he was presently a novice, but because none of its members had ever asked him if he were interested, he assumed that he lacked whatever it took to be one of them.

More striking, however, was Tim's next comment. He told me that when he contacted a member of this same congregation about three years before our meeting to ask about joining, the first question that person asked him was whether he thought he needed more time to be sure about his decision. "I was 31 years of age!" Tim said.

I met Sean recently while visiting his secondary school, where he was vice president of the student body. This young man was in his final year and planned on going to college after graduation. I asked if he had thought about an area of concentration. "Yes," he said, "education. I'd like to be a teacher." I was surprised, having heard that young people, especially young men, were not looking to education as a career; so, I asked him why he wanted to be a teacher. "Oh," he said, in that innocent and natural way some teenagers have, "I've gotten a great deal at this school; I'd like to do the same for other young people."

I inquired about his family's reaction to his decision. He said they were supportive. I asked if he had any siblings. "Four brothers and one sister," came the reply. Believing that grace builds on nature, I thought to myself, here is a young man who might possibly consider religious life. He wants to be a teacher; he's a school leader and appears concerned about others; there is more than one child in the family; and his parents seem supportive of what he wants to do with his life.

Later that evening I asked the members of the community of teaching brothers I was visiting what they thought of Sean. "A great kid," was the unanimous reply. Then came my next question: "Has anyone ever asked him if he wants to be a brother?" The response: silence. Fifteen years ago, many of us would have targeted this young man as a potential postulant for our congregation. Today we don't even raise the question.

Fostering vocations

As mentioned earlier, in many parts of the United States at the moment, a number of religious are pessimistic about vocations and the future of their congregations, and with good reason. We know already that the statistics are unsettling: between 1965 and 2000, the number of religious priests in the U.S. declined from 22,207 to 15,092; sisters from 179,954 to 79,814; brothers from 12,271 to 5,662.[2] Viewing these numbers and feeling a bit overwhelmed by the challenge of vocation promotion that we face today, one wag was prompted to say, "We have tried everything to promote vocations, even prayer!"

But there is still a great deal more that we can do. For example, we are now largely invisible to young people in this country. We can help remedy that situation by opening our communities and sharing our faith and our lives with them. We can also tell them our stories: why we came to religious life, what makes us stay, what joy it brings us. We can invite them personally to consider our way of life as a possibility for themselves. Simply stated, we can be for them what we were meant to be: *Good News.*

We can also work to understand the world in which young people live and by which, to a large extent, they have been shaped. It is not the world from which the majority of contemporary U.S. religious have come. Most of us over age 45 have difficulty realizing that Vatican II and the heady days that followed it are "other people's history" for today's young men and women. The 1980's, not the 1960's, are the touchstone of their reality.

Making sense of our current vocation crisis

There can be no doubt that we have a vocation crisis on our hands, and it is no wonder. Most of us have failed, since Vatican II, to take serious and sustained action to reverse the membership decline in our congregations. Let's ask ourselves this question: what have I done lately, in a personal way, to promote even one vocation to my religious family or to another? For many of us the answer is simple: nothing.

In responding to the current crisis in vocations, our challenge is twofold: to make some sense of it, and to develop strategies for addressing it. As mentioned earlier, some commentators employ a medical model to explain the lack of young men and women in novitiates: they compare religious life to a terminally ill patient.

Others offer a more hopeful interpretation of the facts. They agree that the vocation scene is a bleak one, but suggest that the solution to our current dilemma lies, in part, in a return to many of religious life's past practices. The majority of priests, sisters, and brothers in the U.S., however, doubt that this approach will give rise to a realistic plan of action with which to address the formidable challenge of vocation promotion today.

Suppose, for a moment, that we adopt a third and alternative model to analyze the current vocation crisis. Let's compare present-day religious in this country to a group of missionaries setting out to live among the people of a certain village and engage in the work of evangelization.

At the outset, these missionaries know neither the language of these villagers, nor do they understand much about their culture. Feeling inadequate to the task that faces them, they accept the fact that they have a lot to learn. Since their group is small, the missionaries realize too that, from the very beginning, they must give priority to recruiting new members from among the people of the village.

What can these missionaries do to prepare themselves? They can, first of all, learn the language of the people they are called to serve. Next, they can work to understand and appreciate the culture they are about to join. Finally, they can pledge to put aside a significant amount of their time for the work of vocation promotion.

The missionaries agree to all three tasks, pledging especially to apportion 20 percent of their best time to the work of promoting vocations. Why 20 percent? Because the group members know that if they fail to allot a significant block of time to recruiting new members, they won't have a future and, quite honestly, won't deserve one. Could not the same observation be made about the vast majority of us who are members of religious congregations in the U.S. today?

An oversimplification?

Some of us may be offended by what we judge to be a simplistic and mechanical approach to vocation promotion on the part of our imaginary missionaries. "What about the action of the Holy Spirit?" we wonder, and ask, "Isn't God the source of all Church vocations?"

In recent years, appeals to the action of the Holy Spirit and citing God as the source of Church vocations has become, for some of us, an excuse for contributing little, if anything, to the hard work of securing new members for our religious congregations. God's action is a given in this area; our human efforts, however, are equally important.

God continues to call young men and women to religious life. To foster these calls, we must create within our congregations and Church a culture that promotes vocations, one that helps young people to ask some fundamental life questions: "Who am I? Where did I come from? Where am I going?"

However, if we are serious about helping young women and men listen to God's call and encouraging vocations to our way of life, we will need to do more than foster a congregational and ecclesial culture that promotes them. We must also be missionaries to a group first referred to as "Generation X" or Xers by novelist Doug Coupland. The majority of us who make up today's population of midlife religious neither speak this group's language nor understand its culture and worldview.

No doubt, like the missionaries mentioned earlier, we can learn the language of Xers and come to better comprehend their

143

customs and view of our world. We can also choose to dedicate a significant amount of our best time—at least 20 percent—to the work of vocation promotion. However, we must also answer this larger question: do we have the will to do all three?

Let's assume that we do. To learn the language of Xers and understand their culture, we will need to put on an anthropologist's hat for a short while and set out to visit the land of Generation X. As we do so, let's also try to find some answers to three questions. Who are these people? What do they think about contemporary religious life? What are they asking of it?

Just who is Generation X?

Do you have a ready answer to this question: "Where were you when John F. Kennedy was shot?" Were the Sunday evenings of your childhood made memorable because of radio programs—yes, radio programs—like *The Shadow* and *The Lone Ranger*? Do the phrases "the Catonsville Nine," "the Berrigan brothers," and "Kent State" mean anything to you? Can you recall the Latin Mass, Saturday afternoon confessions, Sodality, Vatican II, a pontiff known as "Good Pope John," and a fast before Communion that started at midnight? If you have answered *yes* to more than one or two of these questions, rest assured: there is little chance that you are a member of that group referred to as Generation X.

Now, try your hand at defining some of the following terms: Beavis and Butthead, break dancing, rap, *Wired,* valley girl, *Tron,* 2 Live Crew, *Reality Bites,* Duran Duran, Leif Garrett, *E.T.,* Atari, safe sex, Swatch, and Tori Amos. For any self-respecting Xer, these phrases, and many others like them, are part and parcel of his or her working vocabulary.[3]

Two fundamentally different sets of experiences have shaped

the worldviews of those of us who are midlife religious and the generation of young Catholics who follow us. If consecrated life is to have a future in the States, we must come to know well the women and men who make up this younger group. They are one of the most important sources of candidates for our congregations.

Meet Generation X[4]

Born between 1961 and 1981, Xers have picked up various contradictory descriptions and labels along the way. Alternately referred to as pragmatic and pathetic, quick and confused, sharp-eyed and unfocused, self-centered and able to step outside themselves and understand just how the world works, they make up the largest and most culturally and ethically diverse collection of men and women in American history. No single type of music, hero, or style of clothing defines them. They number 80 million strong, come in all sizes and shapes, and appear to be more tolerant of diversity than previous generations.

Common traits

Despite their differences, all who comprise the younger generation in this country share a common history that has shaped their outlook on life. From the very beginning of their lives, the message was passed along to them that children are avoidable or, in the case of abortion, disposable. The workaholism and insatiable drive for career advancement and economic success of their midlife sisters and brothers have further convinced many Xers that the well being of children does not rank high among the priorities of an older generation.

Xers are noted also for delaying life commitments and look-

145

ing for a world and Church that will not shift beneath their feet. Is it any wonder? They are the original "latchkey" children; during their growing up years many of them spent more time with the family's television set than with the family itself.

Shopping for busy working parents and caring for younger siblings, a number of Xers took on adult responsibilities at an age earlier than normal. All these experiences helped shape their attitudes toward family, relationships, and life commitments.

So did the fact that Xers paid the price for America's divorce epidemic. During their developing years, they witnessed the collapse of traditional family structures. Back in 1962, half of all adults agreed that people in bad marriages should stay together for the sake of the children; by 1980 less than a fifth held that opinion. America's divorce rate doubled between the years 1965 and 1975.

Over time, then, the men and women of Generation X came to define family without relying on biological ties. For the vast majority of them, relationships rather than blood connections lie at the heart of this social institution. For most Xers, the people with whom they have day-to-day contact and share meaningful conversations and a sense of closeness constitute family. They trust their friendships over all other relationships.

Many Xers want life commitments that will last and are taking their time before settling down. One young man of 20 put it this way: "My father left us when I was 11. In retrospect, I can see now that it was all very adolescent on his part: a new life, a new wife, and a new car. What about my mother, though, and my brothers and sisters, and me? Didn't he care about what happened to us? His leaving continues to have its effects, even now, nine years later. It takes me time, for example, to trust people. I ask myself: 'Can I depend on this person? Will this relationship weather difficult times?' I can't take a chance on life until I am absolutely sure of the ground on which I am standing."

Xers a skeptical group

The life experience of Xers has taught them to suspect institutions. At the same time, they long for a world where people and institutions are who or what they say they are. This apparent contradiction is not surprising. After all, they had their first civics lesson in 1973 watching the Watergate hearings on TV.

Most Xers regard the 1970's as their ideological home. What did that decade teach them? First, to be cynical about grown-ups more skilled at discussing than solving problems. Next, to wonder about an adult world that expressed moral ambivalence when an emerging generation sought clear answers, and hesitated to impose some structure on young people's behavior. Finally, to question a worldview that tolerated a rising torrent of pathology and negativism that was swamping the daily lives of young women and men.

A number of business and political scandals, among them the Savings and Loan and Iran-Contra affairs, coincided with the Xers' coming of age and further fueled their skepticism. As Xers grew into adulthood, the national debt mounted, and incidents of theft and violent crime multiplied rapidly.

In 1980, the men and women of Generation X cast their first vote, mostly for Ronald Reagan. As university students their academic careers coincided with the publication of the report entitled *A Nation at Risk,* warning that education in the U.S. was beset by a "rising tide of mediocrity." A number of public institutions appeared, then, to be fraudulent and dysfunctional. Eventually, many Xers grew distrustful of them and decided that they merited neither respect nor confidence.

Finally, Xers have an antipathy toward social movements. What lies behind this aversion? Their opposition to the 60's idealism of their older brothers and sisters. Young people of that era won many gains for those previously without a voice. The decade failed, however, to achieve many of its promises. One generation's gains eventually became the losses of another.

Championing our high ideals, those of us who make up the Baby Boomer generation undertook organized social actions. With what results for the generation that followed? An AIDS epidemic rather than sexual liberation; nuclear anxiety rather than peace; skyrocketing college tuition instead of low-cost education. Xers quickly came to this conclusion: they had inherited a culture in crisis.

If Xers were invited to stop for a moment, and encouraged to take a closer look at our world and offer some comment on what they saw, they might pass along one observation and at least one piece of advice. The observation? Their generation appears to be the "clean up" crew of this moment in our history. Whatever consequences America must face, Xers will bear the brunt of them. They have already discovered that it will be much harder for them to get ahead than it was for their parents.

Their piece of advice? Contemporary U.S. society needs to put aside its ideological positions and name-calling and let simple things work again. Perhaps this very same message can be applied to our Church and religious life as well.

Technology and Generation X

Technology! Without question, stunning advances in this area over the last quarter century have had a most significant and lasting impact on the character of Xers. Midlife baby boomers might remember the delivery of their family's first TV; most Xers cannot imagine a household without two or three of them.

TV gave Xers a window on a rapidly unfolding visual culture and changed the way in which they acquired information. Many appear to read less and yet seem to know a great deal more than we did at their age. The daily newspaper, once the almost universal source of information about local and world events, has been supplanted in many homes by TV entertainment news, complete with sound bites and carefully crafted visual images.

Over time, along with TV, Xers were introduced to a host of other electronic gadgets: calculators, remote control devices, boom boxes, VCRs, digital cassette players, to name but a few. With the birth of MTV, video also began to imitate reality: alongside real life grew its imitation. A world of popular culture eventually took shape and assumed a number of additional forms: cartoons, comics, clothing, fantasy gaming, and the music and concerts of the young.

Advances in technology gave rise to an information explosion unprecedented in human history. Networking with their contemporaries worldwide, Xers became vicarious participants in the massacre at Tiananmen Square and were "present" at the fall of the Berlin Wall. Over time, many of them began to develop an understanding of the political world's instability. Unfortunately, they did not gain a concomitant sense of hope about this very same world.

Personal computer prices dropped sharply as Xers came of age and skill in using one became the preoccupation of a generation. The PC has probably had a greater influence on Xers than any other technological advance. They spend hours almost every day playing computer games, surfing the net, and visiting its chat rooms, downloading information, and sending and receiving e-mail. The Internet is their second home and there has been no limit to what they have been able to find there.

Xers and the Church

The skepticism that Xers harbor toward institutions carries over to their attitudes toward the Church. Xers, in general, don't take well to conventional religious institutions and prepackaged pieties. They have a deep and abiding suspicion of both. Official "Christianity," in their mind, has become too bound up with U.S. middle class culture. Has the Gospel's radical message been sacrificed, they wonder, so that the dream of middle class white Americans can take precedence? Xers want to reclaim Jesus from the very institutions that assert they minister in his name.

At the same time, a significant number of the men and women of this new generation lack knowledge of many of the basic dogmas of the Catholic faith. Most are doctrinally and historically illiterate when it comes to Catholic tradition. Have a conversation with any number of them and you'll discover quickly that they are neither Catechism nor Council Catholics. Reflecting on her experience as a theology professor at Holy Cross College, in Worcester, Massachusetts, for example, Mary Ann Hindale, IHM, remarked in a recent interview, "You can't assume any kind of cultural background, even with Catholic students, so you begin from ground zero. I didn't think when I got into this 20 years ago that I was going to be a missionary." As if offering support for her observation, some religious congregations today require the few candidates they do have to participate in a local RCIA program early in the formation process.

Xers are not angry with the Catholic Church, just strangely indifferent towards it. They have neither guilty feelings about sex nor bad memories of a Catholic school childhood. As a consequence, the fury that some of us, age midlife and older, direct at the Church perplexes them. They wonder why anyone would remain part of an organization that appears to cause them so much pain and anguish. Rather than hearing about what we no longer believe, Xers would rather learn about what we still hold dear.

Xers and spirituality

Though surprisingly ignorant about many matters of faith and theology, Xers are neither irreligious nor indifferent toward spirituality. The key to their relationship with God, however, will not be found in traditional places. Xers have been forced to search for the fundamentals of their faith in the midst of profound theological, social, personal, and sexual ambiguities. If you want to learn something about their religious interests, hopes, fears, and desires, look to their movies, popular songs, MTV, board games, cyberspace, and television shows.

While spiritually hungry, Xers appear also to be taking their time as they search for a set of deeper human values. They are willing to wait for a credible and authentic vision of life and, indeed, desire one that is compelling and challenging. They hope, too, that when they come across it, some practical guidelines will be included for living it out. Young people are looking for a challenge in this area, one that is demanding along with being inviting and adventurous. They long for something that will ignite within them a passion for life. A rediscovery of genuine Christian tradition, rather than traditionalism, may be a first step toward satisfying their hunger.

Ultimately Xers have a yearning, both implicit and explicit, for an almost mystical encounter with the human and divine. They find the spiritual more readily in personal experience and regard their own as superior to the accounts of others or truths handed down by way of creed or custom.

Tensions between Generation X members and their elders

Thirty years ago, those of us now in midlife were fond of offering this straightforward advice: "Don't trust anyone over thirty." Today, in a strange role reversal, we have shifted the focus of our mistrust to the women and men who have come to be known as Xers. Noticeable tension exists between a number of us Boomers and our younger brothers and sisters.

However, Boomers are not a totally uniform lot. Those of us born on the frontier of Xer territory often enough identify with some of the concerns and worldview of this next generation. With that said, it's also true that for many other midlifers, Xers are a disappointing group, seen as ill-informed, intellectually dull, politically inactive, religiously conservative, and hopelessly materialistic.

Xers, on the other hand, fear that a number of us in midlife are redefining every test of idealism in a way guaranteed to make members of their generation fail. Over time many of them have also made judgments about us, classifying a number of us as nothing more than self-righteous ideologues. Most Xers would be delighted never to have to read yet another commemorative article about Woodstock, Kent State, or Vatican II.

Xers have grown tired of hearing us take credit for things they believe we did not do: invent rock and roll, start the Civil Rights Movement, stop the War in Vietnam, reform the Catholic Church single-handedly with Vatican II. Xers would welcome a little generational humility from us. The majority, though, have given up any hope of seeing just that.

Midlife men and women religious and Xers

Some of us who are midlife men and women religious have been equally unkind to the Xers in our midst, labeling them as reactionary and religiously conservative. At times we experience their presence in the congregation as a threat to the hard-won changes in community life, prayer, and choice of ministry achieved over the past four decades. What a tragedy should the suspicion level about Xers become so great among a few of us that we would risk the future of our congregation's mission rather than admit a significant number of Xers to membership.

Many Xers in religious life find their situation equally oppressive. To begin with, for most Xers Vatican II is other people's history. They experienced neither the pre-Conciliar Church nor its religious life. They tire, too, of being classified as conservative and reactionary when it comes to Church teaching and issues surrounding religious life. One young religious priest, for example, reported frustration with the reaction of his midlife confreres to his criticism of the steps they took after the Council to renew their congregation. "It's sad," he said. "They don't even realize that they threw out the baby with the bath water."

A 35-year-old woman religious reported similar frustration. She framed her dilemma in these words: "I just don't sense in my congregation a movement towards a greater commitment to community, and I need that. I used to think that I was screwed up or somehow lacked personal identity because I wanted community so badly. After all, some of my midlife sisters in the community accused me of being a '1950's wannabe.' But now, I'm beginning to sense that it's okay to want to share my life with others who have the same passion I have, and who are not all older than my mother."

153

Just what do today's young people seek in religious life?

Most young people considering religious life today are looking for two things: a common life and a vibrant spirituality. Once again, they are attracted by the radical possibility of adults trying to live together and so witness to reconciliation and peace.[5] Celibate chastity they can live out on their own, ministry they are doing as Catholic schoolteachers, in parish outreach programs, and through volunteer programs. What they are looking for is community and spirituality.

What encourages them to pursue their interest in religious life? Seeing happy and hopeful men and women religious—people who are truly Good News—and the experience of hospitality extended to them by priests, sisters, and brothers. At a recent conference on religious life, one young participant put it this way to the religious in the audience: "Open your hearts as well as your homes."

Xers with an interest in religious life want to be part of something larger than themselves and to live their lives in a way that makes a difference. They long to give themselves to something that demands passion and commitment. Simply put, Xers considering religious life today want to take seriously what it means to follow Jesus: to serve God in a radical way, a way that can only happen together with others.

They agree that community can be lived out in a variety of ways. But Xers do want to share a life together, in more than a casual way, with others who have the same vision and values. They desire to be part of a community where mutual concern and support and a life of prayer are the foundation of its ministry.

Xers considering religious life as a vocation also want to talk about Jesus, and about prayer, faith, and what it means to have a relationship with God that demands sacrifice. They are confused when they find some of us strangely silent on these topics. Most especially, they want a religious life that demands something of them. If an Xer is going to join a religious community, what that congregation stands for must be worth his or her life.

The life experience of Xers, in general, has left them with two unanswered questions: "Who needs me? What can I contribute?" Without doubt, they are looking for community and a sense of belonging. They long, too, for a simple lifestyle, and some means of expressing a care for the world. Many, in short, are searching for something that will give their lives meaning. We used to call that something "the sacred."

What are young people saying about religious life today?

Ask young Catholics why Xers aren't joining religious life today.

Some will tell you that celibacy is the problem. Many wonder if it is a healthy choice. Others don't want to pass up the chance for a lifelong committed relationship with another person and a family.

Some Xers will remind you that the press reporting on religious life has not been very positive of late. Sad to say, some young Catholics will tell you that, at times, their chief source of discouragement about joining religious life is an individual priest, sister, or brother. You'll be told, too, that as women and men religious we are invisible in the daily lives of the young, or known more by the myths, stereotypes, and television caricatures that still surround our way of life.

A fear of permanent commitments will get honorable mention. Young Catholics will point out that neither parental support nor friends' encouragement is present any more. Whereas in the past a certain prestige surrounded entrance into a novitiate, today many people express dismay when a young person announces such a decision. "Why would you want to do that with your life?" is a not infrequent response.

A number of us in midlife mirror similar attitudes when responding to this question: "What are the greatest obstacles or challenges in congregations today to inviting and sustaining new members?" Our answers? A lack of corporate identity, a failure to be visible, a lack of pride on our part about who we are, an inability to change and accept differences, a lack of hospitality, a tendency to overextend and subsequently to show evident fatigue, tension in the Church, and a failure to invite young people to join.

What about young sisters, priests, and brothers? Do they have anything to add to the discussion when it comes to observations about contemporary religious life? Yes. First of all, hardly perfect people themselves, they assure us that they are not looking for congregations of untainted souls! Second, ask them what attracted them to their institutes and you'll hear the following: the group's clarity of vision, a common life, ministries that respond to absolute human needs, a common focus, and the fact that the Gospel message and a life of prayer are the foundation for the group's life and work together.

They will also tell you that they believe that their Institute's way of life was meant to make its members happy and can do just that. Like some other young people of their generation, they believe that we are called to be Good News. In the eyes of young sisters, brothers, and priests, then, religious life in the U.S. today has potentially something very positive going for it. Unfortunately, a number of other people appear to have missed out on that bit of news. Our collective challenge? To let the Church community and the nation in on what is apparently one of contemporary Catholicism's best-kept secrets.

Millennial Catholics

While the members of Generation X have been the focus of a number of surveys over the past several years, more recently social scientists have identified a new and up-and-coming group in the U.S. whom they refer to as "Generation Y," or the Millennial Generation. Born after 1981, these young men and women will make their presence felt eventually as part of the single largest wave of teenagers in U.S. history—more than 30 million strong.[6] And will those of us who make up the Baby Boomer generation understand this emerging group any better than we did Xers? Yes, but only if we keep in mind these two points: one, that many Millennial Americans will come from families that look quite different than the ones in which we grew up, and, two, that the way in which these young people think will differ from the way in which we thought at the same age.[7]

What are some of the characteristics found commonly among Millennial Americans? To begin with, compared to their Baby Boomer brothers and sisters, the members of Generation Y are, and will continue to be, much more racially and ethnically heterogeneous. In 1976, for example, approximately 85 percent of U.S. teenagers were classified as Caucasian. By the turn of the century, only 67 percent of the country's young people fell into this category. But by the middle of the 21st century, white teenagers will constitute a minority in the U.S.

Among what group is the largest growth predicted? Hispanic teenagers. By 2008 they will outnumber their African-American counterparts. These demographic changes have already had an influence on relationships. Three-fourths of today's Millennial Americans report having friends of a different ethnic origin.[8]

The same demographic shifts have some important implications for religious life, especially in the area of vocation promotion. For example, inviting members of Generation Y to join religious life will, in all probability, change the homogeneous ethnic makeup of many communities, and result eventually in a more heterogeneous group of people. As this shift takes place, the members of these groups will have to ask and find an answer to this question: how do we maintain a spirit of welcome rather than being overpowered by our fear of change?

A second characteristic of Generation Y has to do with family structure. During their growing up years most Millennial Americans will live in families that are smaller than the ones in which we Boomers lived during our early years. And for a very simple reason: unmarried women gave birth to between one quarter to one-third of the children born in the U.S. during the period 1989 to 1994. This development has helped shape new attitudes toward family life among the members of Generation Y. For example, in a recent biannual study of the attitudes of young people, 82 percent of respondents between the ages of 9 and 17 years judged a one-parent home to be as much of a family as a two-parent home.[9]

Third, while Baby Boomers and their parents can take some credit for inventing the generation gap, "Y"s and their mothers and fathers seem to get along well. In the same biannual study cited just above, 94 percent of participants between ages 9 and 17 years said that they trust their parents. Furthermore, 80 percent of those polled reported that they have "really important talks" with parents about their lives.[10]

During the 1960's and 1970's, rebelling against your parents and their values was part of the rite of passage into adulthood. Yes, 30 years ago conflicts about the morality of the War in Vietnam gave rise to bitter divisions in many families. But today no similar great cause lies on the horizon. Rather than rebelling against their parents' lifestyle, most young Millennial Americans—like their counterparts in Generation X—appear worried that they will not be able to achieve it.

Fourth, the men and women who make up Generation Y take choice for granted.[11] By habit they customize everything. Often enough, if something doesn't catch their interest they will use the mouse click of their computer to toss it aside. The world of computer technology, however, may prove to be a mixed blessing for Generation Y. Yes, it will open up endless possibilities of information and learning for each of them. But, with this rapidly developing technology so available, Millennial Americans run the risk of becoming even more individualistic than those who make up the generations that have come just before them.

Some social commentators employ the image of a remote control device to characterize the members of Generation Y, i.e., they are subject to constant change and have a focus that is fragmented. Many Millennial Americans would agree. Change is the only reality that many of them know.

Do these young Americans have anything to say for themselves?[12] Yes, in fact, they do. A number of them are troubled about their generation and describe its members as lacking direction. One young woman summed it up this way, "We feel as though everything is changing and we have nothing to do with it, so we sit back and let it happen."

Other Millennial Americans are troubled that so much has been given to their generation, and so little asked of it. "We don't do anything," lamented one young man. "We don't have any great achievements." In general, then, some of those who make up this emerging generation fear that it fails to stand for anything, that few of its members think for themselves, and that it has no one to look up to, no one in whom to believe.

Despite their less than flattering self-portrait, the members of the Millennial Generation will be worth watching during the years ahead. Many of these young men and women appear to be looking for something more than what life offers them currently; they want to make a difference. Didn't the very same unrest and idealism motivate a number of us to join religious life?

Also keep in mind that along with the forces working on them that are mentioned above, these young adults are also the beneficiaries of stronger and more effective programs of religious education and youth ministry developed over the last decade and a half. A few other pluses. While they grew to maturity, their seniors began to place more emphasis on the care of children and the divorce rate began to slow.

And while some researchers predict that as a group they will be marked more by consensus than self-discovery, and that practicality will matter more to them then creativity,[13] members of the Millennial Generation also are coming of age at a period in our history when interest in religious issues is higher than at any time in recent memory. Teenage Bibles and books on spirituality written exclusively for adolescents are selling well today. While we cannot predict an upturn in applications to religious congregations, we can do our best to directly invite these young men and women to reflect on this question: "Does God's will for me include a vocation to religious life?"

Candidates from among the working class

As mentioned in the Introduction to this book, young men and women from working class and poorer families—including more than a few people new to this country—are often overlooked in discussions about Xers. Particularly evident are immigrants from Asia and parts of Latin America. Those with roots in the Caribbean islands and Central and South America, in particular, face challenges familiar to many immigrants: low paying jobs and many forms of prejudice and discrimination.[14]

To welcome these young men and women more effectively to our institutes, we must, first of all, look closely at the cultures prevalent in our congregations and examine the ways in which we deal with cultural differences and race issues. We must also come to a common understanding about what is entailed in the process of welcoming.

To date, many of our congregations have tended to draw candidates from one or another European ethnic group. By so doing, we have retained certain customs and rituals common to these same groups, further reinforcing our national features.

The languages and cultures of those new to this country, however, often differ greatly from those that characterize the majority of us.[15] A quick look at some characteristics common to the members of our ever-growing population of Hispanic Catholics in the U.S. might help us better understand the point being made here. Expected by many to be the largest ethnic group in the States by the year 2015, Hispanic men and women make up approximately 15 percent of the country's Catholic population today. Consequently, most people predict that this group will be a major force within the U.S. Roman Catholic Church during this new century.[16] It stands to reason, then, that those of us with responsibility for promoting vocations to religious life might look to this group as a potential source of new members for our congregations.

When designing programs to promote vocations among Hispanic Catholics, we need to be aware of those characteristics that distinguish Latinos in our Church from many of their Anglo brothers and sisters. Most of the former have a spiritual life that draws its inspiration largely from outside the framework of institutional structures. Hispanic Catholics are much less likely than

Anglos to be registered members of a parish or to attend Mass on a weekly basis. It stands to reason, then, that if young Latino men and women do not have strong parish ties, the local Church will not be the place to find them. If we truly want to invite and welcome them to our way of life, we must go to those places where they feel most at home.

Keep in mind, too, that Latinos stress personal conscience over the directives of Church leaders when making judgments about the morality of abortion and non-marital sex.[17] Their devotion to Mary is also much stronger than what is usually found among Anglos, reflecting perhaps their attachment to Our Lady of Guadalupe.[18]

Demographics

The current membership of our congregations in the U.S. is approximately 96% Caucasian.[19] And though the population of Latinos, Asians, and African-Americans in the States has increased significantly in recent years, the membership of our groups has failed to reflect these changes. How explain this phenomenon? To begin with, a complex dynamic of unconscious racism and the homogeneous make-up of many of our congregations make it difficult for the members of any minority group to penetrate the rather well-established structures found in so many of our Institutes.

Many younger religious will admit that Latino, Asian, and African-American candidates would find incorporation into their groups difficult.[20] But older members most often insist that they are open to receiving candidates from among these groups. However, these senior religious frequently cannot adapt to the cultural demands that heterogeneity in their congregation would demand.

How can we deal with this challenging situation? Let's begin by taking a look at potential candidates from among Asian and Latino populations. More than a few of them come from families new to the U.S. They bring with them to religious life, therefore, cultures that are rich but different from the dominant culture found in most of our congregations today. A clash of traditions and customs occurs easily when we lack knowledge of these differences.

The meaning of culture

The word *culture* is used to describe the customs and traditions of any group of people. Consequently, when we use the term *cultural differences*, we are referring to the diversity that exists between one group and another in terms of such things as how decisions are made, elders are cared for, and holidays celebrated.

Each religious congregation also has a specific culture which determines how its members do things and go about organizing their lives. If we wish to welcome candidates from among working class and minority families, we will, first of all, need to reflect upon our cultures as congregations and how they influence so many aspects of our life together.

Missionary of the Precious Blood Father Robert Schreiter points out that in welcoming young people from among Latin American immigrant families, members of congregations must be aware of and accept some inevitable cultural differences. If a Mexican-American candidate arrives unexpectedly at the community residence five minutes before dinnertime, accompanied by parents and a brother or sister, and assumes that all are welcome to stay for supper, how does the community react?[21] The members of many groups would be upset that the candidate did not call to say he or she was coming, or to ask about bringing parents and a sibling to supper. In this candidate's culture, however, a prior phone call would not be expected. One is always ready to welcome guests.

Marked differences also exist between the cultures of people from Asia and those of most congregations of women and men religious in the U.S. In general, a number of Asian people new to this country find that questions asked by those of us from the States are much too direct. In often calling for a "yes" or "no" answer, these questions appear to set the stage for a "win/lose" situation. One of the parties involved in the conversation must lose face.

Some from Asian countries are taken aback by what they perceive as the failure of many Americans to anticipate the needs of others. Many of us expect people to ask directly for what they need. Those from Asian cultures generally assume that others will anticipate that they may be hungry, thirsty, or tired.

Atmosphere of welcome

How, then, does a congregation maintain an atmosphere of welcome in the face of cultural differences? To begin with, we all need to realize that the dominant culture in the U.S. is marked by individualism. As a people, we prize individuality and have made the person the center of attention. Latin American and Asian cultures, however, are more typically sociocentric: group solidarity takes precedence over the individual. At the outset, then, we must accept this difference and work to recognize just how it might and does give rise to misunderstandings and conflict.

Next, if we plan on inviting new members to join us, we need to realize that what may constitute a welcome for the majority of the members of our community might be experienced differently by the candidates. People new to the country, for example, often perceive U.S. hospitality as, at first, warm and gracious, but ultimately superficial, leading to some confusion about the nature of the relationship that has been established. What gives rise to the difference in perception here? Many Americans view hospitality as a sign of their general friendliness. People from other countries see it as an important part of a process of building social and personal relationships.[22]

Finally, to effectively incorporate candidates coming from the ranks of families new to this country, we must surrender our implicit belief that the process of formation will iron out any cultural differences and lead to homogeneity in the group. Some long-standing members might say, for example, that by the time these candidates make final vows, they will be just like the rest of us. It does not work that way.

All of these differences can give rise to significant misunderstandings if the community members do not have much experience with intercultural living. Some of us may harbor cultural stereotypes and start to generalize. In the case of our example about the unexpected dinner guests, forgetting that people in any culture have individual temperaments, we might find ourselves saying "all Mexicans are like that." If we wish to attract vocations today, we must put into place education programs that will help all of us move from a place where we deny cultural differences to a place where we accept them as part of every group's identity.[23]

What has been the experience of candidates regarding cultural differences? Most report that while their culture may not be unwelcome, it does go largely unrecognized.[24] Others, however, report experiences that have been quite painful. Candidates need to feel as though they belong. To achieve this end, two things must happen: one, the candidate must feel as though he or she is welcomed and cherished; two, the congregation must commit itself to live with differences in a caring and integrated way.[25] When either element is missing, the outcome is troubling.

One young man whose family was from Latin America put it this way: "What was sad for me was not the fact that the other members of my community knew so little about my language and culture. It is that they had such little interest in learning anything about them." Sad to say, this young man eventually left the congregation of which he had been a member for more than five years.

African-American candidates

Religious congregations that wish to welcome candidates from the African-American community will also need to examine the question of racism within the life of their group. At the outset, two issues must be faced: the racism that exists among the members of the group, and the lack of sensitivity on the part of most of us to the differences between ethnicity, culture, and race.[26]

Let's examine the first issue briefly. Racism is woven into the fabric of U.S. culture. Just ask middle-class African-American businessmen or women in New York who regularly suffer frustration from having one taxi after another pass by them. The number of our fellow African-American citizens imprisoned in state correctional facilities also far exceeds their representative percentage in the general population.

There is little reason to believe that racism is not also present within U.S. religious communities. Our challenge is to find ways to cope with this reality. For a community to say that it will try not to be racist is an insufficient response. We all need to be careful not to deny the racism that exists within our congregations. We must also work to discover how it manifests itself within the group, both individually and institutionally.

The second issue—the relationship between ethnicity, culture, and race—is a bit more difficult to address. Many of us believe that if we are sensitive to cultural and ethnic differences, we will also be sensitive to race. Accepting cultural differences, however, does not adequately address the assumptions of inferiority that are built into racism. These suppositions are embedded deeply in the psyches of whites, and have been reinforced by a long history of subjugating people with a skin color other than their own.[27] Identifying the ways in which our congregations express their racism is a necessary first step toward creating a more hospitable place into which nonwhite candidates can enter.

Vocation promoters' role

Vocation promoters have an important role to play in the process of welcoming candidates from working class families. Their role is critical when these candidates are also new to the country or from the African-American community. The vocation promoter's work must begin with the members of his or her own congregation. The following questions can be of help in getting that process underway. How aware is my group about its culture, its prejudices, and the myths and stereotypes about minorities to which it clings? What is my congregation's level of commitment to inviting and welcoming candidates from the Asian, Latin American, and African-American communities? At the very least, this preliminary work must be done. Otherwise, why invite a prospective candidate into the community? The outcome will only be disappointment all around.

The vocation promoter also needs to work with the candidate. Some important points to consider: for how many generations has the family of the prospective candidate lived in the U.S.? Is he or she first generation—someone who was born overseas and came to the States as a child or adolescent—or have members of the family been in the country for a significant period of time? If the candidate is second generation—born in the U.S. of immigrant parents—he or she must deal with a special set of challenges, particularly the conflict that often arises between the values of his or her parents' culture and those of the dominant U.S. majority culture.

Cultural issues usually play less of a role for minority candidates who are third generation and beyond. There are, however, situations in which a Hispanic candidate, for example, comes to rediscover his or her hispanidad (being Latino). This situation comes about when, faced with the dominant culture of the congregation, the candidate becomes more aware of how he or she is different. That fact alone gives rise to a number of formational tasks centering on the issue of identity.

It is also worth remembering that candidates of Latin American and Asian heritage who have grown up in the States will have already experienced cultural and racial differences to a significant degree. Most have had to face these challenges in school, in the workplace, and in their relationships. Despite this fact, however, many of these candidates fail to grasp the implications of joining an overwhelmingly white community. This issue must be addressed gently with the candidate, but it must be addressed. The same holds true for the community. Throughout the process of formation, both parties—the candidate and the community—must commit themselves to work together so as to negotiate the difficult terrain of cultural differences and race.

As citizens of the United States, we have always lived in a multicultural world. The fact that we have not always fared well in meeting the challenges of this complex situation is evident in the racial and ethnic prejudice that has marked so many chapters of our national history. Even up until the present, many of the cultures that make up our nation continue to live side by side in tension rather than in a spirit of mutual respect.

Today our Church and our religious congregations must face the challenge of becoming more genuinely inclusive. The future vitality and viability of these institutions will depend on just how creative and courageous we are willing to be in finding ways to meet the challenges of multiculturalism and racial diversity in this new century. With that said, let's turn our attention to developing a strategic plan to aid us in inviting and welcoming new members into our congregations.

Reflection Questions

1. If you are middle-aged or older, what qualities do you most admire among today's younger generation? What qualities found in them most trouble you? What are your reasons for both reactions?
2. Now, if you are a member of today's younger generation (i.e., age 40 or below), what is it about today's older generation that you most admire, and what is it that most troubles you about them? Your reasons for both reactions?
3. Do you want a future for your congregation and its mission? What price are you willing to pay—in terms of time, willingness to change some elements of your present life (e.g., ministry, community set-up, style of prayer) to insure that future?

Notes

[1] Parts of this chapter first appeared in *Human Development* magazine and relied heavily on the following sources: Tom Beaudoin, *The Irreverent Spiritual Quest of Generation X* (San Francisco, CA: Jossey-Bass, 1998); Catherine Bertrand, "Vocation Ministry: A Community Project," *CMSM Forum* 70 (Winter 1996), 1-13; Albert DiIanni, SM, *Religious Life as Adventure: Renewal, Refounding, or Reform* (Staten Island, NY: Alba House, 1994); James Gill, SJ, "Why so few vocations? The young

need attractive images to evoke desires," *Human Development* 7(1) (Spring 1986), 20-24; N. Howe and W. Strauss, "The New Generation Gap," *Atlantic Monthly* (December 1992), 67-89; W. Jabusch, "Young and Conservative," *America* 177(10) (October 11, 1997), 5-6; David Nygren and Miriam Ukeritis, *The Future of Religious Congregations in the United States*; W. Wesson, *Generation X: Field Guide and Lexicon* (Los Angeles, CA: Orion Media, 1997); Patricia Wittberg, SC, *Creating a Future for Religious Life*; and Patricia Wittberg, SC, *Pathways to Recreating Religious Communities* (Mahwah, NJ: Paulist Press, 1996).

2   Center for the Applied Research on the Apostolate (CARA Report 2000).

3   Tom Beaudoin, *Virtual Faith—the Irreverent Spiritual Quest of Generation X* (San Francisco, CA: Jossey-Bass, 1998).

4   Ibid.

5   Carolyn Osiek, "A woman religious stands at Mount Nebo."

6   Nathan Cobb and the Globe staff, "Meet Tomorrow's Teens," *Boston Globe,* http://www.boston.com/globe/living/packages/ generation2000/main428.htm.

7   Ibid.

8   Nickelodeon/Yankelovich poll, cited in Nathan Cobb and the Globe staff, "Meet Tomorrow's Teens," *Boston Globe.* http:// www.boston.com/globe/living/packages/ generation2000/main428.htm.

9   Ibid.

10   Ibid.

11   Barbara Schneider and David Stevenson, *The Ambitious Generation: America's Teenagers, Motivated but Directionless* (New Haven, CT: Yale University Press, 1999).

12   Wendy Murray Zoba, "The Class of '00, Part I," *Christianity Today,* February 3, 1997, http:// www.christianitytoday.com/et/7t2/7t218a.html.

13   Neil Howe and William Strauss, cited in Nathan Cobb and the Globe staff, "Meet Tomorrow's Teens," *Boston Globe.*

14   William V. D'Antonio, "Latino Catholics: How different?" *National Catholic Reporter,* http://www.natcath.com/ NCR_Online/102Y/102999p.ht.

15   Robert Schreiter, "Effective Vocation Ministry in an Increasingly Multicultural Church," *Horizon* 25(2), Winter 2000, 22-27.

16   William V. D'Antonio, "Latino Catholics: How different?"

17   Ibid.

18   Ibid.

19   Nygren and Ukeritis, 249.

20   Ibid.

21   Schreiter, "Effective Vocation Ministry in an Increasingly Multicultural Church," 23.

22   Ibid., 24.

23   Ibid.

24   Nygren and Ukeritis, *The Future of Religious Orders in the United States,* 249.

25   Schreiter, "Effective Vocation Ministry in an Increasingly Multicultural Church," 26.

26   Ibid., 24-25.

27   Ibid., 25.

28   Ibid.

Chapter VIII

LAST
CALL FOR
RELIGIOUS
LIFE[1]

A middle-aged married couple had two sons, ages 8 and 10 years. These boys were always misbehaving. Their parents knew that if mischief occurred in town, their children would, more often than not, be at the center of it.

The boys' mother was at her wit's end when, one day, she heard about a local priest who had had some success in changing the behavior of boys like her sons. She telephoned him immediately and asked if he would speak with her two children. The clergyman agreed readily, but insisted on seeing each child individually. The following morning the boys' mother sent her eight-year-old son to the priest's house. The older brother was to follow in the afternoon.

On entering the priest's office the young boy walked quickly towards a chair and sat down in front of an enormous desk, behind which sat the clergyman. A tall and severe looking man with a booming voice, he offered no introduction. Instead, he asked the boy sternly, "Where is God?" The youngster's mouth fell open, but no words came out. He sat there, silent and wide-eyed.

So the priest repeated his question in an even sharper tone.

"Young man," he snapped, "Where is God?" Again the boy gave no answer. Finally, the clergyman raised his voice to a shout, shook his finger at the boy and bellowed, "Where is God?"

Color drained from the boy's face. He bolted from the room and ran directly home. On arriving there, the youngster charged up the stairs, raced into his room, and dove into the closet, slamming the door behind him. His curious older brother cautiously opened the door. "What happened?" he asked.

The younger brother, gasping for breath, whispered, "You and I are in big trouble. God is missing—and they think we are responsible!"

How does this story relate to the task of developing a strategic plan for vocation promotion among our religious congregations in the States today? Whatever motivated the priest in our tale to ask the question he did, the young boy heard it as an accusation. To his way of thinking, he was being held responsible for a situation that was not of his making.

A number of us react in a similar fashion when the question of vocations to consecrated life comes up in conversation. When others point to the current lack of candidates in our congregations, more than a few of us feel as though we, too, are being held responsible for a situation that we did not create. Consequently, some of us become defensive and blame our contemporary culture for our dilemma, or suggest that a younger generation lacks the spirit of generosity so necessary for consecrated life.

Patricia Wittberg reminds us that four incentives fostered vocations in years past: a personal invitation; the enthusiasm and support of family, clergy, and members of the wider parish; the benefits of the life itself; and those "funnels" of new candidates that every congregation somehow managed to organize.[2] As one example of a "funnel," Wittberg points to the particular institutions that many teaching groups maintained that could almost be classified as "feeder" schools to their postulancies. She reminds us also that many of these incentives have been seriously diminished in recent years. Some have disappeared altogether.[3]

The work of establishing a strategic plan to promote vocations to religious life in the States starts with a few fundamental decisions about the nature and purpose of our way of living. These include: clarifying the identity and mission of my religious congregation, establishing a regular rhythm of prayer for vocations, personally inviting young people to join our group or another, and believing that the congregation to which I belong has a future.

In addition, each of our groups needs to make a decision to develop a comprehensive plan of action for recruiting. Such a decision is an important element in any strategic plan for promoting vocations. We begin our work of developing such a plan by taking a look at some of the fundamental decisions that we need to make about our lives as religious today.

Important decisions

In addressing the tasks outlined just above, we must start by determining what we can and cannot do to change some of the elements that are contributing to our current vocation crisis. To begin with, we cannot do much about the current size of families, or the decision of many young people to delay life commitments, or society's growing individualism and materialism. So, too, while we must work to help heal its victims, we cannot undo the devastating effects of past incidents of child sexual abuse. We can, of course, intensify the screening of applicants for religious life, and put into place in our ministries personnel policies aimed at protecting children and young people from abuse.

But there are many things that we can and must do to foster vocations to religious life. First of all, we can pray for vocations, and we can pray daily for this grace. If the work of promoting vocations is to bear any fruit, it needs to be done within the framework of a vibrant life of individual and community prayer.

Second, to invite new members, we must understand the identity of our group and be clear about its mission. We must have a sense of who we are and where we are going. As we have seen, to arrive at that point, we will have to make choices about our congregation's ministry, and its style of community life, and spirituality and prayer. By so doing, we, and eventually everyone else, will understand clearly what our group stands for and what makes it different from others in our Church.

Third, we can also foster vocations to religious life by inviting young people to join our ranks. Have no doubt about it: *our personal invitation to join religious life offered to a young man or woman has been, and continues to be, one of the most powerful recruiting tools we have available.* Unfortunately, today it is also one of the least used.

Fourth, we can take a look at what the social sciences are telling us about vocations. For example, did you know that the current decline in vocations is not solely a Roman Catholic phenomenon? Several Protestant communions are witnessing similar declines among their ordained clergy.

Were you aware of the fact that parental opposition to a religious vocation is not solely a post-Vatican II reality? More than half the women religious surveyed in a 1958 study reported that one or both parents had opposed their entering the congregation of which they were currently a member.[4]

Did you know that a positive family life still carries great weight in fostering vocations? Does it surprise you that attendance at a Catholic school, anywhere from the primary grades through university, but especially during the high school years, also has a disproportionally positive effect on vocations?

Does it surprise you that the men and women religious best able to attract candidates to our way of life are those who have a strong and sacred definition of their vocation, as opposed to those whose definition is more secular?

If we plan to seriously promote vocations, we must also believe that our congregation and its mission have a future. Young people today, understandably, have no interest in joining a group that believes it is going to die in the foreseeable future.

So, too, those of us who make up these institutes need to believe that vocations to our way of life exist in the U.S. today. There is little reason to doubt that they do. The growth of fundamentalist Christian Churches in North America, for example, along with the rapid development of sects, and keen interest in various New Age movements so prevalent in the recent past suggest a profound religious hunger in our society. Our challenge? To develop and implement ways to meet this deep spiritual need.

A strategic plan for recruiting

With the above elements in place, a group with interest in recruiting new members can begin to design its vocation promotion strategy. A clearly formulated and well-implemented plan of action, one that directly involves a significant percentage of our group's membership, if not all of it, is essential for any progress to be made. On local, provincial, and national levels, we need to organize our members into work groups and set up, at least on the local level, regular meetings of these bodies. For what purpose? To allow ourselves to draw up strategic plans for vocation promotion, to implement and evaluate those plans, and to encourage and support one another in the important work of recruiting.

Now for the hard part!

Let's get the difficult commitments out of the way first. What's your answer to this question? Does the mission of your congregation remain as vital and urgent today as it was at the time of your group's foundation, and will it remain so for some time to come? If your answer is "yes," doesn't it stand to reason that every member of your congregation, in light of today's vocation crisis, would want to make the recruiting of new members their number one priority? Vocation promotion is always rightly undertaken for the sake of mission, never, hopefully, for reasons of survival.

First of all, then, if we want a future for the mission of our congregation, we will need to make vocation promotion our number one priority. That's right, our number one priority.

Second, the overwhelming majority—if not all—of our group's membership will need to rearrange other commitments so as to free up twenty percent of their best time to devote directly to the work of vocation promotion. Why twenty percent? Because there is a lot to learn and a great deal of work to be done. If any of our groups choose not to make vocation promotion their number one priority—and we all have that choice— and to provide the time to work in this important ministry, we can reasonably predict that our group will not have a future and, really—as has been stated earlier, it won't deserve one.

We have all heard the litany of very good reasons why this or that member of any congregation just cannot get involved with the work of vocation promotion. Some of us say, "I haven't the time," or protest, "You don't understand the demands that my ministry is placing on me." Others of us hide behind age. "I'm too old," we say. "This work is the responsibility of younger people." Still others excuse themselves with this observation, "We already have a full-time vocation director."

None of these reasons holds any water. Yes, all of us are busy; the median age of a number of our groups would allow the majority of our members to beg off being involved, citing senior citizen status; most of our congregations today have a member full-time in the ministry of vocation promotion. So, let's put aside these excuses and come to a decision. *Do we or do we not want a future for the mission and life of our congregation?*

Action plan for recruiting

Let's continue our planning by taking a look at three of the chief challenges facing us when it comes to vocation promotion. Changing the public's perception of religious life; educating people about contemporary religious life in the U.S.; and beginning again to invite young men and women to join this way of life.

Changing the public image of U.S. religious life

The reputation of priesthood and consecrated life has been tarnished recently because of abuse scandals. The media, from time to time, has also taken note of the rapid and far-reaching changes that have occurred in the lives of U.S. religious over the last four decades. Unfortunately, a number of reports reaching the public have been less than positive in nature. From the "new nuns" of the late 1960's to the empty novitiates and seminaries of today, this consistent message has gone out: great numbers are leaving, few, if any, are joining, everyone is aging. Not a very attractive picture.

Today's media image of consecrated life in the States ranges from the sordid to the ridiculous: abusers of children, religious angry at their Church, congregations divided sharply between liberals and conservatives, the "nuns" of *Nunsense*. Why would any self-respecting young man or woman want to get mixed up with these people? Our challenge: to get out the word that we are a far more varied, complex and happier group of people than our current media image would suggest.

Some concrete suggestions

Make no mistake about it, the image of U.S. religious life that appears in the media has a powerful effect on the view that young people take towards our way of life. Priests, for example, when they are characters on television shows, are rarely seen doing their job. More often than not, they are cast as pedophiles or idiots. A case in point: Fox TV's *Ally McBeal*. One of its programs featured a sexually active nun. David Kelley, the show's writer also created a story line that included a Protestant minister who is prosecuted for his affair with a Church worker. "I realize that doesn't make me an altar boy," the clergyman says to one of his lawyers. "If you were an altar boy," responds the lawyer, "you'd be with a priest." That is outrageous.

Other examples. One, a recent movie, *Jeffrey*, has among its characters a priest who sexually propositions a man in a church sacristy. Two, an advertisement for a student-loan company features a woman religious in a veil with this caption, "If you're a nun, then you're probably not a student." Three, on Jim Lehrer's *Newshour*, a regular Public Broadcasting Services feature, Catholic priests were identified recently as among those most "at risk" for anti-social behavior during a discussion about mandatory DNA testing for criminals.[5]

Though we must make a measured and considered response to these misrepresentations of our way of life, we cannot let them go unchallenged. There is no virtue in remaining silent and strangely passive as religious life is distorted beyond recognition.

There are several steps we can take to insure that theater, films, TV, and the print and electronic media portray our way of life and its members more accurately. First of all, we can correct false and misleading reports when they appear. However, expressing disapproval about media misrepresentations is only a necessary first step. Action is warranted also on another front. We also need to develop accurate and positive stories about our way of life and insure that they appear in the media as often as possible.

Why, for example, did Harlem's Mother Hale and her exemplary and noteworthy work with babies addicted to drugs and alcohol, and those who are HIV positive attract so much news attention, while very similar ministries carried out by women religious usually did not even receive honorable mention?

To change that situation, congregational leaders can challenge the writers, dramatists, and media experts in their midst to use their skills in ways that describe contemporary religious life more accurately. Their efforts can be aimed also at shedding some light on our mission, motivation and spirituality today. Witness the impact, for example, of Helen Prejean, CSJ's *Dead Man Walking,* first a book and later a film.

This effort to present a more accurate and positive picture of religious life needs to be ongoing. A one-time blitz of positive information, followed by a slide back into our present situation, will do little to address long-term the problem we are facing.

In our efforts to transform consecrated life's image in the U.S. media, we can also enlist the aid and expertise of several national organizations. Groups such as the United States Catholic Conference, the Leadership Conference of Women Religious, the Council of Major Superiors of Women, the Conference of Major Superiors of Men, the National Religious Vocations Directors Conference, and Religious Brothers Conference can be of considerable help, particularly in coordinating national efforts to influence the media.

What additional steps can we take to improve the image of U.S. religious life today? One, we can set up local, regional, or national press offices in our congregations or offices at all three levels. Their job? To alert the media about any newsworthy stories involving men and women religious and their ministries.

Two, in years past, there were always a few pamphlets in the rack in church vestibules that explained something of our lives as a sister, brother, or religious priest. Today, such material is notable by its absence. It needs to be developed again and made available in a variety of languages.

Three, while many young Catholics may not be found in the vestibules of churches, they are frequent visitors to cyberspace. We need to use the Internet more effectively to get out the good news about our congregations and to invite young people to join us. In but one example, the Diocese of Providence, Rhode Island has begun to use MTV and opened a Web site (www.catholic priest.com) to boost recruitment for the priesthood. Diocesan officials initiated this effort after asking high school students how they could better reach out to teens and young adults. Another Web site worth visiting lists congregations of men and women religious throughout the world (www.vidimus dominum.org).

Also, writing in the January 16, 2000 issue of the *New York Times*, reporter Lisa Foderaro described the effective ways in which the Sisters of Mercy of the Americas are using the Internet and other means for promoting vocations to their congregation. Having been challenged by their leadership team to recruit 100 young women a year so as to insure the congregation's vitality and viability, the group currently has 23 candidates, 15 novices, and 19 temporarily professed sisters.[6]

Four, our congregations, individually or in concert, can produce some short videos aimed at educating Catholics and the public at large about consecrated life today. In a bolder move, several congregations, or the national religious conferences working together, might approach commercial television producers with ideas for programs that would accurately portray our life and ministry. A TV mini-series with an interesting story line and featuring contemporary men and women religious and their ministries would go a long way toward improving the image of our way of life in the U.S.

Five, we can work at developing a positive relationship with the media. Just how? By establishing contact with our local radio and TV stations and offering to be of help with the religious programming undertaken by these groups. Don't wait for the personnel at a station to suggest to you the idea for a story or interview. Generate those ideas yourself and offer them freely. Don't get discouraged, though, if your ideas are not met initially with enthusiasm. Eventually, some will work out, in light of your objectives and the overall programming goals of the station.

Finally, the voices of young religious need to be heard. At times, it appears as though we, their elders, are willing to listen to everyone else's voice except theirs. To give them such a voice, congregations working together could develop a video series similar in format to the CMSM project, *Men Vowed and Sexual: Conversations about Celibate Chastity*. That series was produced several years ago to help men religious talk with greater freedom and ease about sexuality and their lives of celibate chastity. We have all heard entirely enough about the "graying" of religious life. Giving ear to those new to our way of life, and learning more about their hopes, dreams, and concerns, would benefit us all. One such effort along these lines has been the inauguration of a newsletter entitled *Giving Voice,*[7] which provides a forum where sisters under 50 years of age can share ideas and be mutually supportive.

A video series featuring young religious would also provide parishes, schools, and youth groups with another tool for the work of vocation promotion. Viewers would learn quickly about what first attracted these young people to their communities, and, more importantly, what makes them stay.

Many other ideas can be generated that will help all of us with an interest in changing our way of life's image in the media. We will be limited in our ideas only by the frontiers of our imagination.

Education is called for on several fronts

If we feel a bit shell shocked due to the extraordinary changes to our way of life during the last three to four decades, just imagine what the reactions of the average Catholic are like! In recent years, many have felt betrayed by us. They fail to understand, for example, why we no longer staff the parish school, live in the brothers' house or convent next to the church, or act like some religious of old. Little substantive work has been done over the last few decades to educate the Catholic population at large about contemporary religious life. We need to remedy this situation.

Then, too, a well-designed in-service program about religious life aimed at lay men and women is urgent for a very different reason: everyone in the Church community has a responsibility for recruiting new members for religious congregations: bishops, priests, and laity, as well as men and women religious.

Parents, as we have mentioned, at one time were among the greatest allies religious had in recruiting new members for their congregations. Today these efforts are hampered because so many parents are confused about religious life, its nature and purpose, and the way in which it is being lived out. We must make an effort to restore their trust and enlist their aid once again. Education about the reality of contemporary religious life is a necessary first step in that direction.

If young Catholics and their parents need education about religious life, so also do lay people in general. To meet that need we can offer to teach an adult education course on the topic in our parish, write an article for a diocesan publication, preach at Mass, or give a Lenten or Advent series of lectures on the subject. The means are not quite so important as the message: religious life is alive and well and in need of new members. Armed eventually with a more accurate understanding of U.S. religious life and a greater knowledge of its mission, lay people will be willing to help with efforts to recruit new members for this way of life.

Frank talk about celibate chastity

Celibate chastity is one area where education is sorely needed. Why? Because celibate chastity is in trouble today. Young Catholics, for example, cite it as a possible explanation for the decline in vocations to religious life. Recent reports of child abuse and other sexual scandals involving men and women religious have also led a number of people to question whether a life of celibate chastity is a healthy way for people to live out their sexuality.

Other people wonder whether a life of celibate chastity leads eventually to stunted emotional and psychological growth, or is an impediment to deep and loving relationships. Obviously, a great deal of education about celibate chastity is needed to correct misunderstandings about this way of being a sexual person.

We have only ourselves to blame, though, for some current misconceptions about celibate chastity. Many of us, for example, when asked why we choose to live out our sexuality in this manner, reply with stock answers: for the sake of the Kingdom, to be more available, to love everyone and not just one person. Then, we take a deep breath and hope that no one else asks any more questions.[8]

Most people who question us about celibate chastity do so out of curiosity. After all, only a small percentage of the world's population chooses to live out its sexuality in this way. In responding to their questions, three points need to be made clear.

First of all, celibate chaste people are not asexual. Similar to conjugal chastity, celibate chastity is a particular way of being a sexual person.

Second, the spiritual life must be at the core of any life of celibate chastity. If it is not, this way of living the Gospel makes little sense to others and, eventually, even to those professing to live it. And three, what is needed to live a life of celibate chastity well is pretty much what is needed to live any life well: discipline, asceticism, solitude, and a sense of humor.

Young people, in particular, can ask some pointed questions about a life of celibate chastity. They are curious, too, to learn whether we are faithful to what we have promised. Integrity—being who we say that we are and making choices about our behavior based on our values and commitments—is critical here.

We will be more at ease in talking about our lives of celibate chastity if we develop a vocabulary with which to do so. So, too, more honest conversation about the topic among ourselves can help.

In the final analysis, however, it is the place of intimacy in our lives, and not necessarily genital sexuality, that people wonder about when they express curiosity about celibate chastity. The best response to concerns in that area is the presence within religious life of well-balanced people with dear friends and an ability to relate easily with others.

Invite, invite, and invite!

When the investment-banking firm, Merrill Lynch, is looking for new people to help staff its equity department, it does not send its recruiters to the Fashion Institute of Technology in New York City. Rather, it targets graduating classes at some of the nation's finest business schools and actively seeks out applicants for the positions that it has on hand. As we develop strategies for gaining new membership, we can learn a great deal from the recruiting strategies of corporations.

In recent years, a number of us have reported that older candidates, some quite advanced in years, are more the norm with our groups. One must wonder if the median age of applicants is increasing, however, because the aging members of many of our congregations are spending less and less time with young people. Doesn't it stand to reason that we will attract older and not younger candidates if most of our time is spent with older men and women?

We may be surprised by the fact that a significant number of young Catholics judge themselves as unworthy to join our congregations. They believe they lack whatever it takes to live this life well. By taking the initiative to invite qualified young people to consider religious life, we can help reduce their anxiety and reassure them that they do, in fact, possess those qualities necessary for religious life.

Some of us, though, raise an eyebrow when the conversation turns to today's young people. We are similar to middle-aged parents who, enjoying their retirement and faced with the possibility of their adult children moving back into the family home, begin to see their offspring as a nuisance. If any of us considers young adults to be nuisances, we need to realize that they are very *necessary* nuisances indeed! What about those of us who feel uncomfortable around young people? Often enough, our lack of ease is due to the absence of communication skills useful when relating to the emerging generation. These skills, however, can be learned.

The next step

So what is the next step in inviting young people to join in the adventure of religious life? We must go to those places where generous young Catholic men and women can be found today. And just where would that be? In volunteer programs and Catholic youth groups, on the faculties of Catholic universities and among their student bodies, at Newman Clubs, on parish and diocesan retreat teams and the faculties of Catholic elementary and secondary schools, among the members of parish councils and similar groups, and in service programs. These are natural places to find them. So, too, are organizations such as the Peace Corps, VISTA, and the branches of the armed services.

As men and women religious we have always believed that grace builds on nature. In the past, we identified young people with solid human values and helped them discern whether or not they had a vocation to religious life. There are, as mentioned just above, large numbers of generous young people today, working in a number of volunteer and paid positions with Church, public social service, and educational organizations. We need to learn to spend time with them in all those places and to extend a personal invitation to them to join religious life.

Where they have been neglected, vocation promotion efforts must be re-established in secondary schools and universities, and in parishes. A modern version of the "vocation club" can be set up, posters and written literature about religious life should be visible and available, and there needs to be regular contact between the religious on the staff and the students.

We need, for example, to get out of administrative offices and back into the classrooms of the schools in which we continue to serve today. Alternative positions such as campus minister, counselor, or school chaplain would also give us much needed contact with students. We need to be close to young people if we are ever to be in a position to invite them personally to join today's religious congregations.

Parish communities can also be the source of vocations. *Called by Name*, a program that asks parishioners to identify from among the young people of their local community those with the qualities needed for religious life, is but one example of how the local Church can help with the ministry of vocation promotion. We are well advised to take advantage regularly of this type of program.

Other initiatives

Along with addressing the three main challenges outlined above, there are a number of additional elements that we can include in our congregation's pastoral plan for vocation promotion. We can, for example, set up some new ministries with vocations in mind. In the past, most of our groups have done just that. Consider, for example, the academies established by congregations of women and men in the last century with the purpose of attracting the most capable Catholic students. From among their number, they hoped to attract new members. Likewise, today we need to locate at least some of our ministries in those dioceses with sizable Catholic populations with the plan of recruiting from among this group.

In evaluating our commitment to certain long-standing ministries, we would benefit from identifying those that continue to provide our congregation with vocations and those that do not.

If a particular work should be producing vocations and is not, we should ask ourselves these two questions: "Is there anything more we can do to encourage vocations among the young people of this area? If not, for what reasons do we continue our commitment to this work?" If we have done all that we can to encourage vocations in a particular ministry, and none are forthcoming when it seems that they should be, we better have some other very good reasons to justify our decision to stay with that work.

Another way of looking at permanent commitments

In working to turn around the current downturn in vocations, we can also challenge the conventional wisdom about permanent commitments. Xers are reluctant to put down roots. Their hesitancy is due, in part, to what they observed during their growing up years: the disintegration of the American family and the collapse of some revered institutions. Many also believe that they will be freer if they "keep their options open." This notion is mistaken.

Permanent commitments are quite compatible with freedom. Real freedom, after all, means self-determination. What better way to achieve that end than to put down roots? We need to help young men and women discover that fact anew.

We also need to help them understand that there are some commitments in life for which the word "forever" is appropriate. Marriage is one of them; so too is commitment to religious life. What justifies such commitments in our day and age? To date, no better way to grow has been found than to put down roots.

Age of commitment

As we develop a pastoral plan for vocations, we can also revisit questions about the most appropriate age at which to welcome young people into the process of initial formation. Subsequent to Vatican II, the vast majority of religious congregations in the U.S. made a decision to delay the age at which candidates could enter the postulancy or novitiate. Conventional wisdom suggested that young men and women were better suited for formation after they had completed university studies and, perhaps, worked for a few years. Based on the belief that it would insure greater maturity in candidates, the decision to delay the age of commitment was popular.

Admitting a candidate to religious life at an older age, in and of itself, however, has no apparent bearing on his or her ability to manage difficulties and stress in later life.[9] In contrast, personal identity, that sense of who a person is and where he or she is going in life, does help one to cope with the inevitable stress that accompanies growth and change. Delaying the age of commitment of candidates to religious life, though, in no way insures that they will achieve a solid sense of personal identity.[10]

The decision to accept candidates at a later age also brought with it a number of additional and unexpected problems. Those showing an interest in religious life at the end of secondary school, for example, were now subjected unchallenged to the best and worst aspects of American culture for several more years. Many of us believed rather naively that we could undo the negative influences of the culture and re-educate candidates into Gospel values once they entered formation.

The time has come to take a hard look at the successes and failures of formation programs that were inaugurated after Vatican II. Without a doubt, these initiatives introduced many welcome changes in the process of initiating new members into religious life.

They have also, however, discouraged a number of young people about this way of living out the Gospel message. One young man put it this way, "It is almost impossible to join some religious congregations today. The ones I've looked into keep encouraging me to wait and to take advantage of a 'normal experience of development.' It makes me wonder what they think about their own life together. Also, I am beginning to question whether they have any interest at all in having me as a member."

A return to pre-Vatican II formation programs is not the answer. However, those instituted subsequent to the Council do not appear to be working the magic that they promised. Today we would do well to ask ourselves some pointed questions: Is it possible that a nineteen or twenty year old person knows his or her mind sufficiently that admitting him or her is, in fact, the right move? Do we need to develop a more highly structured program of formation for university students with an interest in religious life, one that aids candidates to form a better sense of personal identity? What helpful models of vocation discernment can we develop for young people in this particular age group?

Has the time come, for example, for religious congregations to set up houses of discernment? These centers would aim to help potential candidates take a serious look at this way of living out the Gospel. Made up of vowed members working in ministry and some young people, also fully employed, such groups would have to be clear about their identity and be marked by a regular life of prayer and service. Members would commit themselves to building an adult community of believers in the tradition of the founder or foundress of the congregation in question. The young people involved would be expected to live a life similar to that of the vowed members and would participate in regular spiritual direction. After a year or two of living with such a group, a young man or woman would hopefully have a much better idea about the Lord's dream for him or her.

With the steadily increasing median age of our congregations in the U.S., we must also ask ourselves this question: do we persist in delaying the age of commitment of candidates to our groups because we would just as soon not have a collection of unfinished and unruly nineteen and twenty year olds underfoot? Young people can disturb midlifers and their seniors with their questions and challenges. Their presence, though, is also a rich source of new life and energy.

Generation X and religious life: Are we willing to invite them in?

While Boomers did not single-handedly reform and renew U.S. religious life, they did make a contribution. The generation of priests, sisters, and brothers now classified as middle aged came to this way of life thirty to forty years ago with ideas that many of their elders judged unorthodox. While those religious Boomers helped move along the winds of change that were sweeping over religious life in general, their most significant contributions came eventually in the area of mission.

Many of them numbered among those who challenged the members of their religious congregations to return to the original spirit of their foundresses and founders and to respond to the Church's call to have a special concern for the poor. By asking some hard questions, they forced the members of their groups to take a close look at what they were doing and just why they continued to do it.

While Xers will also have something helpful to say about mission, the major contribution that they can make appears to lie in two other areas: community life and spirituality. Mission, community, and spirituality form the backbone of religious life. While Boomers have not ignored the last two, they have given special attention to mission. Members of the current younger generation are making us mindful of community and spirituality. We need to welcome their contribution, remembering how difficult our questions about mission were to some in the generation that preceded us.

For example, Xers make us uncomfortable when they challenge some of the community arrangements that midlife religious have grown to accept as the norm over the past three decades. Their questions about spirituality, Jesus talk, prayer and faith worry many contemporary and middle-aged women and men religious because, in the past, such a primary focus could easily degenerate into a "me and God" type of religion. Perhaps, though, the questions that these young people pose about prayer and faith can help point us toward a genuine apostolic spirituality, one that moves us away from the monastic forms that have been passed down to us and on to new ways of praising God. Actually, rather than witnessing the death of apostolic religious life today, we are, instead, being asked to live it out in a very new and dynamic way. The members of Generation X can play an essential role in this adventure.

A final point. Lest we idealize the emerging generation, let's admit that some of them can be maddeningly self-centered, hypercritical, and self-righteous. Aren't those the qualities, however, that make young men and women so interesting and exasperating, all at the same time? Today's young people, like their counterparts in the generations that preceded them, are unfinished. The process of formation is intended as a challenge to help them grow. It goes without saying that if we invite them in, we will have to face a number of very difficult situations. Some of them will be unsuited for religious life, others will need more time to mature. Still others, though, are destined to be fellow travelers with us on this pilgrimage that religious life was always meant to be.

American ingenuity

As Americans, we are a pragmatic people. Some would suggest that, as a nation, we have never doubted our ability to solve a problem. Let's, then, give ourselves this challenge: ten years to turn around the current vocation crisis among religious congregations in North America. We have seen that the media, used effectively, can be a powerful ally in our efforts to get out the good news about this way of living out the Gospel. We have also suggested that men and women religious will need to learn to talk more openly about their spirituality and lives of celibate chastity, and establish designated communities of welcome and discernment while fostering the same spirit in their remaining houses.

Permanent commitments, the age of admission to religious life, ongoing education for laity and clergy: all these areas need to be revisited and, where necessary, action plans developed to address them. Additionally, congregations need to choose some new ministries with vocations in mind, establish stronger links with young people from the working class and minority groups, and teach their members, once again, how to ask young men and women to join them. Most importantly, a significant number of us must free up twenty percent of our time for the work of vocation promotion.

Vatican II challenged men and women religious to undertake a revolution of the heart. We must realize, however, that we don't have to be extraordinary to accomplish this end. Instead, all that anyone of us has to do is to live well our day-to-day lives. Have a spirit of welcome, be patient, practice forgiveness, love others, listen well, be tolerant, withhold judgment, be willing to go that extra mile. Simply put, be a brother or sister in word and deed. Could we ask for a better advertisement for religious life, in our day, or in any other?

The hour grows late for a number of congregations with members in the U.S. We have little time to waste, and our groups will be dead if we wait for all our members to be "on board" before embracing the radical type of transformation called for by Vatican II and subsequent Church documents. Rising to meet the challenge of vocation promotion now, at the dawn of a new century, let's begin our efforts by re-igniting the fire that must burn brightly at the heart of our way of living. It is passion, after all, that has always attracted the young to religious life. Rest assured, it will do so once again.

Reflection Questions

1. Spend some time developing a pastoral plan for vocations for your province or region.

    Begin by examining what is in place already. Perhaps your group has a more than adequate plan, and you just need to find your role in it.

    Where no plan exists, begin to develop one by asking yourself this question, "Who are we as a congregation and for what do we stand?" Also ask yourself this question: "What message do we wish to communicate about our group and its mission?"

    Now, decide at whom you will aim this program, e.g., young women or men just out of secondary school, those who have finished some college or graduated, young single lay teachers in the schools where members of your congregation serve, other young people working in the agency, hospital, parish where your group is represented. How can you most effectively reach them and how can you best communicate your message?

What other groups in your geographic area do you need to target for education about religious life and renewal, e.g., parents, pastors, those who serve alongside you in ministry? Identify each of these groups and decide how best over the next twelve months to bring them up to date on what has happened in religious life during the past 40 years, and what your congregation has been doing to adapt and renew itself.

What about the media image of religious life in your geographical area? Do religious priests, sisters, and brothers have a positive image among those who make up the Catholic community, and those who make up the wider community? If yes, what can you do to maintain that positive image? If no, what steps can you take during the next calendar year to change the situation?

What gifts or skills do you have personally that can be used in the work of vocation promotion (e.g., an ability to write well, an ease in relationships, artistic talent)? How specifically can that talent be used during the next twelve months to further vocation promotion for your congregation and/or other groups?

What other elements need to be included in your province or region's pastoral plan for vocations?

Notes

[1] Parts of this chapter first appeared in *Human Development* magazine and drew from the following sources: Catherine Bertrand, "Vocation Ministry: A Community Project," *CMSM Forum* 70 (Winter 1996), 1-13; Neil Howe and William Strauss, "The New Generation Gap," *Atlantic Monthly* (December 1992), 67-89; William

Jabusch, "Young and Conservative," *America* 177(10) (October 11, 1997), 5-6; David Nygren and Miriam Ukeritis, *The Future of Religious Congregations in the United States*; Patricia Wittberg, SC, *Creating a Future for Religious Life*; and Patricia Wittberg, SC, *Pathways to Recreating Religious Communities* (Mahwah, NJ: Paulist Press, 1996).

2   Patricia Wittberg, SC, "What to expect from Generation X."

3   Ibid.

4   NCCB Committee on Vocations, *Summary of Vocations Research*, http://www.nccbuscc.org/voctions/resrch/summary.

5   James Martin, SJ, "Anti-Catholicism in the United States: The Last Acceptable Prejudice?" *America* 182:10 (March 25, 2000), 8-16.

6   Arthur Jones, "New Mercies for a New Era." *National Catholic Reporter* 36:16 (February 18, 2000), 15-19.

7   For additional information about *Giving Voice*, please contact: *Giving Voice*, c/o Jackie Hittner, RSM, Sisters of Mercy, 605 Stevens Avenue, Portland, ME 04103-2691, USA.

8   See Seán D. Sammon, *An Undivided Heart.*

9   Seán D. Sammon, *Relationship between Life Stress, Level of Ego Identity, and Age of Commitment to Central Life Structure Components in Age Thirty Transition Catholic Religious Professional Men* (Doctoral Dissertation, Fordham University, New York, 1982), and Seán D. Sammon, and Marvin Reznikoff and Kurt F. Geisinger, "Psychosocial Development and Stressful Life Events among Religious Professionals," *Journal of Personality and Social Psychology* 48:3 (1985), 676-687.

10   Ibid.

EPILOGUE

Mary Ward got it right. She accepted the fact that new beginnings are usually fraught with difficulty. In 1609, this young Englishwoman and a small band of her followers traveled from their homeland to the Spanish Netherlands. There they began to educate young women who numbered among the English Catholic émigrés escaping persecution at home.[1] The Jesuits were doing as much for the young men of the region. But, contrary to the conventional wisdom of her day, Mary knew that women were as capable of education as men.

Mary Ward's dream of establishing a community of women based on Jesuit principles was not welcomed by all. "Wildly innovative" was the phrase that some Roman authorities used to describe her. And throughout her life the number of prominent clerics who opposed her efforts—for reasons that had nothing to do with religion, or even good sense—always outnumbered those who supported her.

But Mary Ward's community grew. Its members established school after school. Finally, the powers that be decided to domesticate this new charism. So, they made her an offer, instructing her to choose one of four pre-existing rules for her sisters. Oh, but there was a catch. All four rules, as applied to women at the time, required canonical enclosure. To choose any one of them would bring a stop to the work she and her "English Ladies" had been called to do.

And so Mary Ward resisted. And matters got worse. She suffered at the hands of a less than candid Pope Urban VIII, and was accused of heresy and imprisoned. Her followers were driven out of their houses; many were on the verge of starvation.

Released from prison in 1631, Mary traveled to Rome to clear her name. Subsequently, she returned to England where she continued to work with her community until she died in 1645.

After her death, Mary Ward's Institute—the Sisters of the Blessed Virgin—flourished. Finally, in 1977, after a wait of 366 years, Mary's sisters were able to realize her original dream. With the blessings of the then Superior General, Pedro Arrupe, they adopted the Jesuit constitutions.

New beginnings

Why begin this Epilogue with the story of the life and struggles of Mary Ward? For this simple reason: to illustrate that new beginnings are not easy. Mary was given the grace of beginning a religious institute. Today, we have been given the grace of helping our congregations to begin again. And, like Mary Ward, we have discovered that responding to that challenge is neither simple nor easy. If, at times, the task has been demanding, the problems formidable, and the journey discouraging, why are we surprised? New beginnings are most often fraught with difficulties.

This book has presented one view of the state of consecrated life in the U.S. today. It has also identified some of the challenges that we, as men and women religious, must face if we are to be agents of God's renewal of our way of life at this time in its history.

Vatican II challenged us to live out a dual fidelity by returning to the spirit of our founders and foundresses, and taking action in response to urgent and unmet human needs. But if truth be told, despite extensive studies of the spirit of founding persons and a great deal of talk, more than a few of our congregations in the U.S. have been somewhat restrained in responding to the Church's call to renew and adapt consecrated life.[2]

So, while a great deal of good will and hard work has gone into ensuring the renewal of religious life in our day and age, a great deal also remains to be done. Our challenge at this point in time is not so much to rein in a number of groups who have gone too far in their efforts to renew, but rather to challenge the many more of us who have failed to go far enough.

When faced with the possibility of radical change, many of us demonstrate ambivalence about moving forward. In part, this response is the result of our fear of personal conversion. But philosopher Bernard Lonergan, SJ reminds us that religious conversion is akin to an "other-worldly falling in love. It is total and permanent self-surrender without conditions, qualifications, reservations."[3]

The journey of renewal initiated by Vatican II invited us to embrace such a process of conversion, knowing full well that the transformation of consecrated life would depend upon the presence of people motivated by faith more than anything else.[4] Who else could take on the thankless task of disturbing people, of pointing out the gap that exists between what we profess and the reality of our lives? Our failure to take the steps necessary to radically transform our congregations and works stands in stark contrast to the spirit of adventure and risk taking that marked the birth of so many of our groups.[5]

Today, we also have on hand the experience of 40 years of experimentation with religious life. Let's admit that we have gathered enough data to identify at least some of the fundamentals that will characterize a vital and viable expression of our way of life for the 21st century. By so doing, we can use what we have learned to fashion new forms of religious life suitable for our time and place in history.

A crossroad

As U.S. religious we stand at an important crossroad today. Traversing it safely will require that we answer this question adequately: what must we do to ensure a vital and viable future for our congregations and their mission? Without doubt, Jesus figures in our answer. He and his Gospel must have their place at the center of our lives as men and women religious. It is Jesus who will ultimately move us to do generously that which we must do.

Second, we must also admit that the renewal questions of the year 2002 are not those of 1965.[6] Consequently, some customs that served us well over the past three to four decades may now be nothing more than a hindrance to the ongoing adaptation and renewal of consecrated life in the U.S. Do we have the courage to look fearlessly at that possibility and to make any necessary changes?

Third, the simple, and yet difficult, act of listening must mark any process that hopes to move the work of renewal ahead with satisfying results. And these few ground rules might help us ensure that the act of listening is one of the hallmarks of our work. One, let's be careful not to surround ourselves only with people who share our outlook, and, two, let's make a commitment to read more than just those publications that support our opinion about the place and purpose of consecrated life in our Church and world.

Yes, it would be easier not to have to sort through various points of view. However, if we are to arrive at new understandings about religious life and its identity, we cannot simply do what is easy. We will have to do what must be done to achieve the goal that we have set for ourselves.[7]

Leadership

And what about the role of leadership in our present situation? Here again, Mary Ward provides good example. She was the quintessential "sidewalk manager," understanding the importance of presence. Despite her delicate physical constitution, she went back and forth across the Alps, mostly on foot, frequently in winter and in the midst of the Thirty Years War, strengthening and encouraging her followers. Like Moses of old, she went from tent to tent with interest, a word of encouragement, and, at times, a challenge to change.

Religious leaders today, like the women and men who founded their congregations, can do no less. Memos and written statements have their place in the life of any group, but they are a poor substitute for the physical presence of leaders who define themselves as brothers and sisters among their brothers and sisters.

And what must the leader do today? Three things. One, keep the vision alive. Two, tell the truth. Three, be a herald of hope. Let's look at each in turn.

The primary task of any leader is to keep the vision of the group alive. If he or she does not, who will? And where can that vision be found? In the Word of God and the institute's Constitutions.

But today's religious leaders must do more than give definition to their group's vision. They must call all of us to live out, as radically as possible, the ideals of our congregation.

Two, as a leader, always tell the truth. You don't have to tell all the truth all at once, but it's important to always tell the truth. People respect, even welcome, honesty. After all, dishonesty is patronizing. As a leader, then, call the shots as you see them. And don't worry about making mistakes. People are more forgiving than we might imagine.

Three, be a herald of hope. It's easy to be pessimistic, but not very helpful. Consider Winston Churchill. During the Second World War, when the people of Britain had little reason to hope, and invasion and defeat at the hands of Nazi Germany seemed inevitable, this man single-handedly rallied the spirit of the nation. Though the situation in which U.S. consecrated life finds itself today is hardly comparable to Britain during the last World War, leaders in religious life can learn something from Churchill's approach. Communicate a confidence in God's presence and guidance, a conviction that your group has a future, and a challenge to the membership to be as generous and involved as possible in the congregation's life and its mission.

Our congregations have resources that would have stunned the men and women who founded them. These courageous individuals were heralds of hope in much more trying situations. So, let's not wring our hands, but continue to work to renew our way of life in the Church. And let's also invite a new generation to join us in the adventure of religious life.

The Promised Land

How privileged we are to live at this time in history, and in the history of consecrated life! Yes, we have passed through a long night since Vatican II, and we have suffered great losses. The poverty that is our lot today, however, may allow us to admit at last that, in the end, renewal must be God's work.

Carol Osiek, RSCJ, writing in the February 18, 2000 issue of *National Catholic Reporter*, had this to say about religious life and Vatican II: "Those of us who remember Vatican II... thought we had arrived in the Promised Land."[8] "And, indeed, there was ample justification for that reaction. The Church began to implement liturgical reform. Canon law was to be brought up to date, and Protestants were benignly referred to as 'our separated brethren' rather than as heretics. Most importantly, laymen and women began to feel that perhaps they did have a genuine place in our Church after all."[9]

Forty years of efforts to adapt and renew religious life in this country have taught us that our task may be to traverse the desert but not to take possession of the Promised Land. Moses didn't. He died in the mountains just outside Canaan. His mission as a leader was to help God's Chosen People make the passage. Ours might very well be the same: to prepare the way for those who come afterwards.

Yes, during the four decades since the Council, we have learned that the journey will be longer than we expected, the challenges greater than we imagined, the work involved more taxing than we had anticipated. But we have already come a long way, and the future is in sight if we only have the heart and will to bring it to life.

If we look carefully and honestly at all that is transpiring in religious life in the U.S. today, we will discover that we have much for which to be thankful. We will realize, too, that some difficult decisions lie ahead about the shape and form of our ministry, community life, and the manner in which we praise God. But God is with us, and we have our talents and resources, and the gifts and good will of God's people to aid us. And so, in a spirit of hope and with cautious optimism, we can say that a new day is about to dawn for our way of life in this country and that, yes, it is morning for consecrated life in the U.S. once again!

Notes

1 The details about the life of Mary Ward are taken from an article by Lawrence F. Barmann, "Mary Ward: Centuries her Scroll," *Review for Religious* 59:6 (November/December 2000), 608-616.

[2] Nygren and Unkeritis, *The Future of Religious Orders in the United States*, 244-251.

[3] Bernard Lonergan, *Method in Theology* (London: Herder and Herder, 1972), 240ff.

[4] Gerald A. Arbuckle, SM, "Understanding Refounding and the Role of Conversion," in Gerald A. Arbuckle, SM and David L. Fleming, SJ, eds., *Religious Life: Rebirth through Conversion* (Staten Island, NY: Alba House, 1990), 66.

[5] Nygren and Ukeritis, *The Future of Religious Orders in the United States*, 244.

[6] Garvey, "Almost any group?"

[7] Dirk Dunfee, SJ, "Both the rascals and the prophets can be the voice of God," *National Catholic Reporter* 36:22 (March 31, 2000), 2.

[8] Osiek, "A woman religious stands at Mount Nebo."

[9] Ibid.